# cooler than chillies

# cooler
# than
# chillies

## Lesley Waters

## with photographs by Gus Filgate

HEADLINE

First published in 2000
by HEADLINE BOOK PUBLISHING

10 9 8 7 6 5 4 3 2 1

Cataloguing in Publication Data is available from the British Library

ISBN 0 7472 7490 8

Frontispiece: *Black and Red Stew with Avocado and Soured Cream* (see page 18)
Page 7: *Melon with Peppered Parmesan* (see page 91)

Designed by Isobel Gillan
Illustrations by Amanda Patton
Printed and bound in Italy by Canale & C.S.p.A.

HEADLINE BOOK PUBLISHING
A division of the Hodder Headline Group
338 Euston Road
London NW1 3BH

www.headline.co.uk
www.hodderheadline.com

## For Mum and Dad with all my love

### Acknowledgements

It has been a real pleasure putting together *Cooler Than Chillies*. Much of this is due to Louise Wooldridge who has worked so hard, has the patience of a saint and keeps me in constant check. I cannot thank her enough.

Huge thanks also go to Anna-Lisa Aldridge for all her enthusiasm, time and work on the book.

I wish to thank Heather Holden-Brown and Lorraine Jerram at Headline for their continued support, and my editor Susan Fleming who once again was always ready with unfaltering encouragement, help and advice.

Thanks again to Gus Filgate, Maxine Clark and Penny Markham for the brilliant photography and special thanks to my agents Fiona Lindsay and Linda Shanks for their guidance.

Finally to my husband Tim for always being a true taste critic – what a brave man!

This symbol, which appears at the bottom of some recipes, indicates where meat or fish can be added to a dish.

# contents

Introduction • 6

*The Chosen Spice: an A–Z* • *8*

*Caring for Your Spices* • *13*

*Spice Bump and Grind* • *14*

Chilli Chill • 15

Out of the Ground • 37

Sowing Seeds • 60

Popping Pods • 79

Bush Berries • 90

Bark and Blossom • 100

Mixed Spice • 116

Spicy Sips and Supplements • 130

Sugar and Spice • 142

Index • 158

# introduction

*Cooler Than Chillies* is a continuation of my passion for the modern approach to vegetarian food. Like me, more and more people are discovering vegetarian food and just how far it has come. By the day, it increases in popularity, and I believe it takes a major place in modern healthy eating.

I have always loved combining different styles of cuisine and, of course, with their versatility, chillies and spices play a major role in this. Whilst spices can be hot and kicking, they can also be warm, aromatic, gentle and subtle. Twenty years ago, for many people, spicy food was either a burning hot chilli con carne or a vindaloo curry, but in modern cooking, used on their own or blended together, spices are the perfect ingredient for creating fresh, vibrant flavours and stunning, everyday, healthy food.

So, what is a spice? The dictionary definition is 'an aromatic and pungent vegetable substance used as a condiment for seasoning food'. They come in many forms and can be berries, seeds, bark or pods, and they can be fresh or dried. Spices are cultivated and used all over the world, from the cooler regions of Europe to Central America, the West Indies and all over Asia. Spices have been around since ancient times, and were used not only for cooking, but for medicines, fragrances and even embalming! They have always been a valuable ingredient, and are still grown, sold and eaten worldwide today, with pepper being the most popular and important in most countries. In Britain at one time spices were so expensive that, like jewels, they were kept under lock and key by the lady of the house.

If you have never cooked with spices before you will be amazed at how they can become so much part of your everyday cooking. The more you eat, the more you use, and the more you want! *Cooler Than Chillies* tells you how to buy, store and prepare these little precious jewels, and then how to transform them into fantastic food for breakfast, lunch, tea, dinner and, of course, not forgetting puds. You may even find that, like some friends of mine, you'll enjoy them so much you'll be sprinkling chopped chillies on your food in place of salt and pepper. *Cooler Than Chillies* aims to be a happy addiction!

*Lesley Waters*

# THE CHOSEN SPICE: AN A–Z

**This is by no means the ultimate encyclopaedia of spices. It's simply a collection of facts and information about my favourite spices, the ones I frequently use and which are featured in this book.**

## Allspice berries

These pea-sized berries are grown mainly in Jamaica, picked from the allspice tree, a member of the myrtle family. Available whole or in ground form, their flavour is a combination of nutmeg, cinnamon and cloves, hence their name. Allspice is widely used in sweet and savoury recipes, especially in Jamaica, where it features in all manner of dishes from stews to jams and biscuits.

Grind the berries in a pestle or mortar or in your own special spice grinder.

## Caraway seeds

An umbellifer, therefore related to the carrot and parsley, caraway seeds were very popular in Elizabethan times. This is the spice that gives rye bread its distinctive flavour. If stored correctly as a whole spice, it will hold its essential flavouring oils well. Beware of cooking it for too long, as this will impart a bitterness to a dish. The leaves are not eaten. The seeds are best used whole.

## Cardamom

Cardamom belongs to the ginger family, and was originally used as a perfume. It is almost as expensive as saffron and vanilla, so buy the dried cardamom seed pods and grind the seeds and pods as required. (You may want to discard the husky pods, but most of the time I never bother.) Green cardamom pods are the best for flavour (white pods are simply bleached green pods), and you can occasionally find large brown pods (from a related plant, but not so pleasant in flavour). Cardamom is used in Scandinavia for flavouring cakes, pastries and breads, and you can also try chewing the highly aromatic seeds to freshen your breath!

## Cayenne pepper

Cayenne is the fine pepper ground from a fiery chilli pepper variety, along with its seeds. The name is probably derived from the capital of an area of French Guiana, where the peppers grew. Cayenne is very hot stuff, so use it sparingly or to taste. It can be put on the table as a fiery condiment.

## Chilli peppers

Hundreds of species of chillies are now grown worldwide. Originally from Central and South America, the Spanish are credited with introducing them to the rest of the world in the sixteenth century. Chillies can now be bought fresh, ground, flaked or in whole dried form. Members of the capsicum family (as are sweet or bell peppers), chillies vary in shape, size, colour – from unripe green to the riper red and yellow – and strength. As a general rule the larger, rounder, fleshier varieties are not as bitingly hot as the tiny, skinnier, spiky varieties. However, the only sure way to tell is to taste them!

Always buy plump, unwrinkled chillies, and for less heat discard the seeds and innards. Cut the fresh chilli in half lengthways and wash away the seeds under cold running water. Cut into strips – and a good tip here, do this from the fleshy inside as it cuts more easily than the shiny skin. To prepare dried whole chillies, simply crush. You can rehydrate them slightly by soaking in boiling water to soften, then you can grind them to a paste or chop more easily. Remember to wear gloves or wash your hands thoroughly after handling chillies; if you don't, and touch any sensitive part of your body, you may experience great discomfort. If you are desperate to cool down after eating a hot chilli, water is *not* the answer! Try a yoghurt or milk drink or a cold beer which will be far more effective for diminishing the heat. And as a final warning, chillies are addictive. The more you eat, the more you'll want!

## Cinnamon

Cinnamon is a warm, sweet spice used in savoury and sweet cooking. From Sri Lanka, it is the inner bark of a tree of the laurel family. The bark can be bought rolled into quill-like sticks or in a ready ground form. Do not confuse cinnamon with the inferior cassia, a thicker, rougher bark from a similar tree. This has a more robust, coarser flavour. The sticks are great used whole or broken up in sugar syrups, mulled wine, in rice and couscous dishes, and in curries. Powdered cinnamon is good sprinkled over pastries and milk puddings before serving, and is delicious on thick, hot, buttered toast!

## Cloves

Cloves are the dried flower buds of a tropical tree. They are available whole or ground, but I have found that it is better to dry-roast and grind them yourself into a coarse, pepper-like powder. Clove is a very atmospheric spice that never fails to remind me of winter nights, Christmas, hot mulled wine and baked golden, clove-studded apples. Cloves can be used in sweet or savoury dishes, and because of the numbing quality of the essential oil, have even been used to treat toothache.

## Coriander seeds

The coriander plant produces both herb leaves and spice seeds. The seeds have a very different flavour to the leaves popularly used in South-East Asian, Indian and Mexican dishes. The seeds can be bought in whole or ground form, and are a main ingredient in many curry powders, pickling spices and *à la grecque* dishes. They are also one of the flavourings in the famous Benedictine liqueur. Coriander seeds have a slightly orangey taste, but this is not too overpowering, and it is a spice that can be used generously. Gently dry-roast the round seeds, then grind or bruise, or even leave whole, depending on the dish.

## Cumin seeds

Cumin is a musky, powerful spice and, like coriander, forms part of most curry powders. Usually found as light brown oval seeds or in a ground form, there is also a black version which is smaller and sweeter. Cumin looks quite similar to caraway, but the flavour is very different. Sometimes Asian recipes list caraway in the ingredients, but this is generally a mistake and should read cumin. Dry-roast the seeds, and use whole or ground.

## Dill seeds

Dill is a an umbellifer, a member of the parsley family, and produces both the herb fronds and the seeds. In medieval times the seeds were said to be used in love potions, but they have a slightly bitter flavour, and are now popular in pickled-type food, especially in Scandinavia and eastern Europe. Crush lightly to release the flavour, or use whole – good in dressings and soups etc.

## Fennel seeds

According to folklore, fennel seems to cure everything from stomach wind to bad eyesight! Fennel is grown in two forms: sweet fennel, which produces the feathery herb fronds and seeds; and Florence fennel, which is the bulb vegetable. All have a subtle liquorice flavour and contain anethole, which is used to flavour drinks such as pastis. The seeds are best used whole.

## Galangal

Galangal is a member of the ginger family, a rhizome, and is similar in appearance but more spindly. It is slightly stripy and translucent, and has a pinkish tinge. There are two types of galangal, greater and lesser. Greater galangal is popular in Thai cooking, and is the larger of the two. It is available fresh and dried. Lesser galangal is smaller and is used more or less as a vegetable in Asia. Prepare both as you would ginger (see Ginger), although they have a much shorter fridge life and only keep for a week or so.

## Garlic

Garlic is reputed to have many medicinal powers, amongst them helping to prevent heart disease, acting as an antiseptic and warding off vampires when worn as a necklace! Whole fresh garlic bulbs are generally hung and dried after harvesting, and have an intense flavour. This becomes milder with cooking, especially when the cloves are roasted whole, before squeezing out the cooked purée inside. Garlic can be bought as a purée, powder, flaked or as salt, but none of these are a proper substitute for the real thing.

Many people use garlic crushers, but personally I find you lose half the garlic in them (and the crusher often goes green and mouldy even after washing up). Because garlic is so smelly, I use a separate wooden board for chopping it. A large bladed knife is essential. I crush the individual clove of garlic with the flat of the blade, after which the skin comes off easily. Then I sprinkle on a little salt and use the sharp side of the blade to 'mash' and 'chop' the clove into a pulp.

## Ginger

Ginger was one of the first oriental spices to reach Europe and to be widely used. It is said to be excellent for the digestive system, relieving sickness and even treating the plague! Ginger is a rhizome, or type of underground root, and a whole fresh root is known as a 'hand'. It should always be bought when plump and firm. Fresh ginger will last in the fridge for several weeks but it can also be bought dried, ground, pickled, preserved in syrup and crystallised. This versatile spice gives a fresh heat to dishes but in a very different way to chillies. It is suitable for sweet and savoury use, and can even be found as a tea or wine. To prepare fresh root ginger, peel the skin away with a small sharp knife, and chop finely or grate if you prefer. You could also bruise it and infuse it in liquid or oil.

## Horseradish

Horseradish is native to eastern Europe and is a member of the cabbage family. It looks rather like a parsnip, a root growing underground with a head of lustrous green leaves above. Once planted, it spreads like wildfire, almost like a weed. It was originally used in Britain as a medicine, and only relatively recently has it become the popular accompaniment to roast beef. Horseradish, although not often available fresh, is an excellent source of vitamin C. It has a very hot, pungent flavour, much of which is lost when it is cooked. It can also be bought in relish or creamed form, ground or grated in jars. To prepare a fresh root, peel with a small sharp knife, then grate. Hard work, but worth the effort. It's so pungent that it will have you weeping in your mixing bowl!

## Juniper berries

Juniper berries are the fruit of an evergreen shrub, and are well known for giving gin its distinctive taste. Use the back of a spoon to lightly crush the berries before cooking to release the essential flavouring oils. Juniper works well with cabbage, potatoes and beans, in conjunction with rosemary, and is popular in pickles and marinades.

## Lemongrass

Lemongrass is an oriental grass with a bulbous base, and is an essential spice in South-East Asian cooking. It has a distinctive lemon smell and flavour, and is now much more readily available in fresh form. Prepare it by discarding the tough outer leaves, and chopping or bruising the inner section. Fresh lemongrass freezes well, or it can be bought in brine, dried and ground. Use it sparingly in these latter forms.

## Liquorice

Liquorice, a bushy plant which is widely grown in Europe and Asia, was once a speciality of Yorkshire, the home of Pontefract cakes. It is the dried and crushed root of the liquorice plant that holds the sweet, distinctive flavour. Familiar for its use in cough medicines, for cooking it can be used in sweet and savoury dishes (though I have favoured sweet dishes, see Sugar and Spice). You buy it in glossy black stick form which is very concentrated and firm; slice and infuse this in liquid, and it will dissolve. You can also buy and melt Pontefract cakes. Liquorice is occasionally seen as a twig-like root, which children used to love to chew long ago – who needs toothpicks!

## Mustard seeds

Mustard has always been widely available and popular in cooking and medicine – mustard plasters were once used to treat arthritis. The seeds can be black, brown or white, the black and brown having more flavour, but none of them have any smell. Different mustard seeds, crushed or uncrushed and with or without husks, are blended to make various pastes and powders sold as English, Dijon or grainy mustards. For most dishes, prepared mustards are the best; if using the seeds in curries, they can be heated and popped in a little oil or dry-roasted.

## Nigella seeds

Nigella seeds come from a plant closely related to the blue flower, love-in-a-mist, and have a light peppery, spicy taste. They are commonly used in Indian food. They are often called black onion or cumin seeds, but spice purists say nigella is different, with a superior taste. In my featured recipes, any will work, so use whichever you can get!

## Nutmeg and mace

Mace is the lacy aril or covering of the nutmeg, the fruit of a tropical tree. Mace is also the more expensive of the two. Although they are part of the same plant, nutmeg has the stronger and mace the gentler, some say better, flavour. Being more subtle, mace is associated with milky, buttery, creamy, often rich foods. It comes whole, and is best infused in liquid such as milk, or you're more likely to buy it powdered as it is very hard to grind at home. Nutmeg is said to be an aphrodisiac and stimulant, and is always best freshly grated. Invest in a special little nutmeg grater and grate as needed. Brilliant when used in egg, cheese and spinach dishes, or added to mulled drinks.

## Paprika

Paprika is widely used in Spain and Hungary, and is probably most famous for lending its flavour to Hungarian goulash. Available in mild, sweet or hot form, it is made by drying and grinding to a powder a special variety of red sweet or bell pepper, usually without the seeds. The mildest versions are ground without the veins. Treat paprika with care in cooking, as it burns easily. It's worth investing a few extra pennies in buying the best quality paprika. Use it up quickly as it has a very short shelf life.

## Peppercorns

All peppercorns are the fruit of a tropical vine, in different stages of development. Green peppercorns are the unripe berries, which are picked and used fresh (rarely seen here), dried or preserved in brine (rinse the latter well). The flavour is milder than black or white. Black peppercorns are the unripe berries, which are picked and dried in the sun until hard and black. Their flavour is more pungent than green or white – and I'm afraid the only way I can describe them is that they're very peppery! White peppercorns are the ripe pepper berries, which are red in colour, with their outer skin removed, then dried. They are less aromatic, more subtle than black. Pink peppercorns are either ripe vine berries (rarely seen here) or, sometimes, the berries of a South American tree. Eaten in large quantities these latter berries can be toxic.

## Poppy seeds

The slate-blue poppy seeds used in cooking are harvested from the opium poppy, but the ripe seeds have no extra effects! Yellow and brown seeds can also be found. Poppy seeds are delicious on bread or in dressings, and in Indian and Turkish dishes are crushed to a paste and used as a thickening. If I am using them in salads or dressings, I like to dry-roast them first.

## Saffron

Saffron is the most expensive spice in the world. It consists of the hand-picked stamens of crocus flowers, and it takes over 5,000 stamens to give 25g (1 oz) in weight! Saffron gives a beautiful, creamy yellow colour to food, and an unusual, aromatic and unyielding flavour. Bought in thin threads or strands, it is steeped in warm water to release its colour and flavour. It is also available in powder form, but as this can be adulterated, I would avoid it.

## Sesame seeds

Sesame seeds are from an annual plant which originated in Asia. They have a very warm nutty taste and, like poppy seeds, are popular sprinkled on loaves of bread. Black, white and brown seeds are available. The oils from unroasted seeds are widely used in the production of margarines, whilst the roasted seeds make a darker oil used in oriental cooking. The most famous sesame product is probably tahina, a paste which is delicious in dips such as houmous. Look out too for a Japanese seasoning which is a mixture of black and white sesame seeds and dried flakes of salted seaweed – you scatter this on top of anything you fancy!

## Sichuan peppers

The Sichuan or anise peppercorn is actually a berry, and is a very old Chinese spice. It is a main ingredient in the Chinese five-spice powder. It is aromatic and fruity in flavour, with some heat, and gives a strange numbing sensation in the mouth similar to that of the clove. Before using the berries, they should be dry-roasted until just smoking, and then ground.

## Star anise

Star anise is the dried pod of a small tropical evergreen tree. Similar to anise as its name suggests, it is star-shaped, and contains seeds in its eight points. Star anise has always been a main ingredient in Chinese cooking, and is a constituent of Chinese five-spice powder. It was used in Britain in the seventeenth century in jam making, and its distinctive flavour can often be recognised in cough medicines. Infuse the pod and seeds in a liquid such as a syrup, a tomato sauce, a wet marinade, curry sauce or vegetable stew.

## Tamarind

Tamarind is a pod containing pulp and seeds, the fruit of the tropical tamarind tree. It can be bought as a mass in a block, or sometimes strained and reduced in a concentrated form. The block of pulp needs to be soaked before use. Very popular as a souring fruit flavour in curries, in some parts of the world it is also enjoyed as a drink with sugar and water, rather like lemonade.

## Turmeric

The turmeric rhizome or root, also known as Indian saffron, is actually related to ginger. It has bright orange flesh, which gives dishes a distinctive yellow colour and has even been used as a fabric dye. It is sometimes used as a cheap alternative to saffron, but has a gentle heat and its own distinctive, warm aromatic flavour. The turmeric generally available has been boiled, dried and ground to a powder. Very occasionally it can be found fresh and used grated, which gives a much lighter, spicier taste.

## Vanilla

Vanilla is the seed pod of a yellow orchid vine, native to Mexico. The pods are picked and cured to allow their flavour to develop. The cured brown pods have a sweet, strong aroma, and when used whole in custard or cream-style dishes, can be washed, dried and used again. Many dishes call for the seeds to be scraped out of the pods. If you can't find the pods, be sure to only use vanilla extract, and not the inferior vanilla essence, as a substitute.

## Wasabi

Wasabi is also known as Japanese horseradish, though it is no relation to European horseradish. Wasabi is bright green in colour and has a pungent heat and flavour. Buy it in ready-to-use paste form or as a powder and mix up like English mustard.

## CARING FOR YOUR SPICES

**Many years ago, when I had my first flat, I had a spice rack on the wall, in the sunniest, hottest position, with the dried spices stored in pretty glass jars. Fashionable this may have been, but for my poor spices it was a death sentence! Spices need to be treated with care and here are some basic rules.**

## Dried spices

Dried spices, especially already ground, have a short shelf life, about three months for ground and six months to a year for whole. So check the date before and when you buy them, buy them in small quantities, and do regular stock checks. Spices like dry, cool and dark conditions. So don't store them on your windowsill or wall, but in a dark, cool cupboard, in airtight jars, away from direct sunlight.

## Fresh spices

Fresh spices such as ginger, horseradish, lemongrass and chillies can be stored in the salad drawer of your fridge for about two weeks. Or for longer storage, for up to three months, prepare the first three spices as described, and freeze in user-friendly quantities. Garlic stores well hung or stored in a cool dry place.

## Bottled and jarred

Fresh spices can now be bought on their own or in blends in jars. Purists would shun these, but they make excellent emergency standbys. Normally preserved in oil or brine, once opened, store in the fridge and use quickly.

# SPICE BUMP AND GRIND

In order to release the essential oils of a spice, and thus the full flavour, dried whole spices usually have to be ground or at least bruised. Preparing and grinding dried whole spices such as peppercorns and seeds is a hard job and needs a heavy hand! Berries, pods and fresh spices need a softer touch, though. One or more of the following is a must if you're serious about getting spicy!

## Sharp knife and chopping board

A simple way of preparing fresh spices such as chillies, lemongrass, garlic and vanilla pods.

## Graters

For grating ginger or horseradish. To freshly grind nutmeg, use either the smallest hole on your cheese grater or invest in a special nutmeg grater with will probably have a little compartment for storing your nutmeg.

## Rolling pin

Use to bruise and crush soft spices such as lemongrass, ginger, soft berries and pods.

## Pepper mill

A very simple but effective grinding apparatus for dried spices, but not very practical when it comes to cleaning.

## Pestle and mortar

A mortar is a heavy, sturdy, bowl-shaped dish with a heavy, thick bulbous implement, the pestle, for pounding. Probably the most versatile piece of equipment, they are excellent for hard spices, pounding pastes or crushing soft berries. Available in clay, stone, marble or wood, they range in size and price.

## Mini food processor

Great for whizzing up pastes, spice blends, dressings and sauces. Easy to clean, and versatile.

## Coffee grinder

A coffee grinder makes an excellent dry spice grinder, but keep it only for spices or your coffee may begin to taste very strange! Can be difficult to clean; try brushing out with a pastry brush.

## Electric spice grinder

These are an expensive option, but do the job efficiently and effortlessly.

# DRY-ROASTING

Many spices benefit from being dry-roasted to bring out the flavour, before being added to the main dish. To dry-roast, simply gently heat a heavy-based pan and add your spice. Toast ground spices, stirring and shaking, over a medium heat for about 30 seconds until the aroma is just released. Whole spices and seeds will take a little longer but be careful not to burn your spice, or it will taste bitter and be unusable.

# NOTE ON RECIPES

All the eggs used in this book are medium.

# chilli
# chill

From fresh to dried chillies, cayenne to paprika, this is the largest chapter in the book. Hot and spicy to cooler and more gentle, so versatile are chillies that here you will even find a *Chilli Sorbet with Tequila*! The classic spicy food, chillies are always a great favourite.

# CORNBREAD SALAD WITH FRESH TOMATO SAUCE

*Sweetcorn kernels combine with hot chilli peppers for this New England style cornbread. Serve on crisp lettuce and dunk in fresh tomato sauce.*

serves 6

butter to grease the tin
280g (10 oz) cornmeal or fine semolina
85g (3 oz) plain flour
2 teaspoons bicarbonate of soda
salt and black pepper
1 egg
150ml (5 fl oz) milk
425ml (15 fl oz) buttermilk or natural yoghurt
1 × 400g (14 oz) can of sweetcorn, drained and rinsed
1 × 115g (4 oz) jar of chilli peppers, drained and chopped
4 tablespoons chopped fresh parsley

FOR THE TOMATO SAUCE:
225g (8 oz) ripe tomatoes, roughly chopped
2 tablespoons sun-dried tomato paste
2 tablespoons olive oil
a pinch of caster sugar
1 bunch of fresh coriander, roughly chopped

TO SERVE:
1–2 baby gem lettuces, broken into leaves and washed

1 Preheat the oven to 200°C/400°F/Gas Mark 6. Generously butter a shallow tin or a small roasting tin of approximately 25cm (10 inches) square.

2 In a large bowl combine the cornmeal, flour and bicarbonate of soda, and season well. In a jug combine the egg, milk and buttermilk.

3 Pour the contents of the jug into the bowl of dry ingredients and lightly combine (do not over-stir, as this will cause the cornbread to be tough). Stir in the sweetcorn, chopped chillies and parsley.

4 Pour the batter into the greased tin and bake in the preheated oven for 25–30 minutes until firm and golden on top.

5 Meanwhile, place all the sauce ingredients in a food processor, season well with salt and pepper, and whizz together.

6 To serve, cut the warm cornbread into pieces, sit each serving on some crisp lettuce and serve at once with the fresh tomato sauce.

(V) Serve the cornbread, without the tomato sauce, with steaming fish chowder or grilled scallops.

# CHILLI SORBET WITH TEQUILA

*Serve this fantastic sorbet as a starter or a pud. It's even better when presented in salt-rimmed glasses.*

### serves 4–6

280g (10 oz) caster sugar
850ml (1½ pints) water
juice and zest of 5 limes
2 fresh red chillies, de-seeded and very finely chopped
2 egg whites
tequila (or vodka)

1 Place 225g (8 oz) of the sugar and the water in a saucepan. Gently bring to the boil, dissolving the sugar, and simmer for 10–15 minutes until a light syrup is formed.

2 Add the lime zest, juice and chillies and transfer to a shallow freezer-proof dish. Place in the freezer until just frozen.

3 In a large bowl, whisk the egg whites to soft peaks, then whisk in the remaining 55g (2 oz) sugar. Turn the frozen mix into a food processor with the egg whites and whizz briefly until just combined.

4 Return the mix to the shallow dish and place back in the freezer until completely frozen.

5 To serve, divide the sorbet between four chilled glasses, and pour a shot of tequila over each. Serve at once!

# BLACK AND RED STEW WITH AVOCADO AND SOURED CREAM

*Avocado and soured cream is the perfect dressing for this spicy black-eye bean stew. See photograph on page 2.*

serves 4

1 tablespoon sunflower oil
1 large onion, chopped
1 large red pepper, halved, de-seeded and cut into strips
2 garlic cloves, crushed
2 fresh red chillies, de-seeded and finely chopped
2 teaspoons ground coriander
1 × 400g (14 oz) can of chopped tomatoes in rich tomato juice
200ml (7 fl oz) tomato passata
a pinch of caster sugar
approx. 300ml (10 fl oz) water
salt and black pepper
1 × 400g (14 oz) can of black-eye beans, drained and rinsed
1 bunch of fresh coriander, roughly chopped
4 tablespoons natural yoghurt or soured cream
1 large ripe avocado, stoned, peeled and sliced

1 In a large pan, heat the sunflower oil. Add the onion and fry for 5 minutes until softened. Add the pepper, garlic, chillies and ground coriander, and fry for a further 3 minutes.

2 Stir in the canned tomatoes, tomato passata, sugar and water. Season and bring to the boil. Reduce the heat and simmer for 15 minutes, adding extra water if it becomes too thick. Stir in the black-eye beans and simmer for a further 10 minutes.

3 To serve, stir in half the coriander and ladle the stew into large warmed soup bowls. Swirl each helping with a little yoghurt or soured cream, and top with the avocado and remaining coriander. Serve with crusty bread.

# BAKED SWEET POTATOES WITH CHILLI SIN CARNE

*The minute amount of chocolate adds an essential richness to this dish. Fantastic with rice or, as served here, with baked sweet potatoes.*

serves 4

4 medium sweet potatoes, washed and pricked
5 dry sun-dried tomatoes
3 large dried red chillies
115g (4 oz) Puy lentils
1 tablespoon olive oil
1 onion, chopped
1 × 400g (14 oz) can of kidney beans, drained and rinsed
1 × 400g (14 oz) can of chopped tomatoes in rich tomato juice
150ml (5 fl oz) red wine
2 garlic cloves, crushed
15g (½ oz) plain continental chocolate, roughly chopped
salt and black pepper

TO SERVE:
soured cream
chopped fresh chives

1   Preheat the oven to 200°C/400°F/Gas Mark 6.

2   Place the sweet potatoes in the preheated oven and bake for about 1 hour or until cooked.

3   Meanwhile, place the sun-dried tomatoes and chillies in a small bowl and cover with boiling water. Leave to stand for 20 minutes, then drain and roughly chop.

4   Cook the Puy lentils as per the instructions on the packet, and drain.

5   In a large pan, heat the oil. Add the onion and fry for 5–6 minutes until golden. Stir in the kidney beans, canned tomatoes, wine, garlic, drained Puy lentils, chopped chillies and sun-dried tomatoes. Bring to the boil and simmer for 15–20 minutes.

6   Just before serving, stir in the chocolate, and season to taste.

7   To serve, split open the sweet potatoes and fill each with some chilli sauce. Finish with a little soured cream and some chopped fresh chives.

# PAWPAW AND PASSIONFRUIT VINAIGRETTE

*A refreshingly different starter or snack to thrill your tastebuds!*

serves 2

> 1 pawpaw
>
> FOR THE DRESSING:
> 3 passionfruit, halved with the seeds and flesh scooped out
> juice of ½ lime
> 1 red chilli, de-seeded and very finely chopped
> 1 tablespoon grapeseed oil
> 1 tablespoon roughly torn coriander leaves

1 Cut the pawpaw in half and scoop out the pips.

2 In a large bowl combine the dressing ingredients together.

3 To serve, place a pawpaw half on each plate and spoon the dressing into the centre well. Serve at once.

# CHILLIED THYME CHEESE

*Try this cheese as a starter or in place of pudding, served with* Cracked Black Pepper and Figgy Bread *(see page 92). Kenyan chillies are generally a little less hot, and don't kill the taste of the cheese.*

serves 4

> 225g (8 oz) goat's cheese (chèvre) or feta, cut into slices
> 1 fresh green Kenyan chilli, de-seeded and finely chopped
> 1 fresh red Kenyan chilli, de-seeded and finely chopped
> a handful of young thyme sprigs
> 1 tablespoon extra virgin olive oil
> black pepper

1 Place the cheese on a serving plate and sprinkle over the chillies. Pull the leaves from the thyme sprigs and scatter over the cheese. Drizzle over the olive oil and lightly season with black pepper.

2 Leave to marinate for half an hour at room temperature.

# GARLIC AND CHIVE PATE WITH NECTARINE AND OLIVE RELISH

*This pâté is a delicious garlicky-chive cheese, which is far better than those you can buy. The olive and nectarine relish cuts the richness and gives it zing – a perfect starter with hot bread.*

serves 4

225g (8 oz) cream cheese
225g (8 oz) ricotta cheese
2 garlic cloves, crushed
1 bunch of fresh chives, chopped
salt and black pepper

FOR THE SALSA:
2 ripe nectarines, stoned and finely diced
2 fresh green chillies, de-seeded and very finely chopped
8 Greek black olives, pitted and finely chopped
juice of $1/2$ lemon
1 tablespoon olive oil

1 Line six dariole moulds or ramekins with non-pvc clingfilm.

2 In a large bowl cream together the cream and ricotta cheeses. Add the garlic and chives and season well.

3 Spoon this cheese mixture into the prepared moulds, pressing it down firmly. Place in the fridge for 4–6 hours.

4 Meanwhile combine all the salsa ingredients together and set to one side.

5 To serve, turn the cheese moulds out on to four plates. Spoon some of the salsa over the top of each and serve at once with hot toasted ciabatta.

# OPEN-ROASTED VEGETABLE PIZZA

*To spice up the pizza, simply add more chilli to the salsa.*

serves 4

1 aubergine
1 large red onion
1 large red and 1 large yellow pepper
3 tablespoons olive oil
salt and black pepper
1 × 145g (5¼ oz) packet of pizza dough mix
½ bunch of spring onions, finely chopped
1 large garlic clove, crushed
1 fresh red chilli, de-seeded and finely chopped
115g (4 oz) cream cheese, mixed with 2 tablespoons water
1 bunch of fresh basil leaves, roughly torn

FOR THE SALSA:
1 × 200g (7 oz) can of chopped tomatoes in rich tomato juice
85g (3 oz) fresh ripe tomatoes, diced
1 fresh red chilli, de-seeded and finely chopped
½ bunch of spring onions

1 Preheat the oven to 220°C/425°F/Gas Mark 7.

2 Cut the aubergine, onion and peppers into 3cm (1¼ inch) pieces. Toss with 2 tablespoons olive oil and season. Roast for 30–35 minutes until lightly charred.

3 Meanwhile, make up the pizza base as directed on the packet, incorporating the spring onion, garlic and chilli. On a lightly floured surface, lightly roll out the dough into a thin round of about 23cm (9 inches) in diameter. Transfer to a baking tray, cover and leave in a warm place for 15 minutes.

4 In a bowl, combine all the salsa ingredients, and season with salt and pepper.

5 Place the proved pizza base in the preheated oven and cook for 10–15 minutes until golden and crisp.

6 To serve, transfer the base to a serving board, and spread on the chilli salsa. Pile on the roasted vegetables and dot over the cream cheese. Scatter with the basil.

Ⓥ Omit the aubergines and top with stir-fried turkey or pork strips.

# PAD THAI NOODLES

*A veggie version of this classic Thai dish. Rice noodles are now available dried or fresh from the chiller cabinet.*

serves 4

115g (4 oz) rice noodles
1 tablespoon sunflower oil
200g (7 oz) sugar-snap peas
1 bunch of spring onions, roughly chopped
2 fresh red chillies, de-seeded and finely chopped
2 garlic cloves, crushed
3 eggs, beaten
4 tablespoons soy sauce mixed with
   1 tablespoon sun-dried tomato paste and
   2 tablespoons water
140g (5 oz) beansprouts
110g (3½ oz) cashew nuts, toasted and roughly chopped
juice of ½ lime
lime wedges to serve

1 Cook the noodles as directed on the packet.

2 In a large wok, heat the oil. Add the sugar-snaps and stir-fry for 1 minute. Cover with a lid, reduce the heat and steam-fry for 1 minute. Then remove the lid and increase the heat. Add the spring onions, chillies and garlic, and stir-fry for 30 seconds.

3 Push the contents of the pan to one side and pour the eggs into the empty side of the pan, over the heat. Cook the egg over the heat, stirring constantly for 1 minute or until the egg is just set.

4 Mix all the pan contents together, pour in the soy sauce, sun-dried tomato paste and water, and heat gently. Drain the cooked noodles and add to the pan along with the beansprouts and cashew nuts. Toss everything together well.

5 To serve, squeeze over the lime juice and pile the noodles into individual bowls. Serve at once with the lime wedges.

 Omit the sugar-snap peas and replace with 225g (8 oz) peeled tiger prawns.

# MEXICAN BEAN CAKES

*Spicy Mexican-style burgers in a bun, which have a really satisfying texture and a chilli kick.*

makes 6

olive oil
1 red onion, chopped
1 large garlic clove, crushed
3 teaspoons ground coriander
2 × 400g (14 oz) cans of red kidney beans, rinsed and well drained
6 pickled chillies, chopped
1 egg, beaten
85g (3 oz) cornmeal

TO SERVE:
6 medium soft white baps
1 large avocado, stoned, peeled and sliced
6 tablespoons good-quality tomato relish
150ml (5 fl oz) soured cream
1 bunch of fresh coriander leaves

1  In a frying pan, heat 1 tablespoon of the olive oil. Add the onion and fry for 5 minutes until softened. Add the garlic and ground coriander and cook for a further minute.

2  In a large bowl, roughly mash the beans. Add the onion mix, chillies and egg and mix together well. Shape the mixture into six cakes and dip in the cornmeal, using your hands to press on the cornmeal and form a coating. Transfer to the fridge and chill for at least 30 minutes.

3  To cook, shallow-fry the bean cakes in olive oil over a medium heat for about 8 minutes until crisp and golden brown, turning over once. Drain on kitchen paper.

4  To serve, place a bean cake in each bap and top with avocado slices, tomato relish, soured cream and coriander leaves. Serve at once.

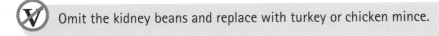 Omit the kidney beans and replace with turkey or chicken mince.

# CHILLIED EGGS ON CRISPY ROCKET SALAD

*Eggs and chilli are a great combination. The egg yolks should still be runny so that when cut they 'ooze' over the rocket leaves!*

serves 4

2 slices focaccia bread, diced
4 tablespoons olive oil
1 tablespoon lemon juice
salt and black pepper
1 fresh red chilli, de-seeded and cut into fine slivers
2 spring onions, halved and cut lengthways into fine slivers
4 eggs
1 × 85g (3 oz) bag of rocket leaves or rocket salad

1 Preheat the oven to 220°C/425°F/Gas Mark 7.

2 To make croûtons, toss the bread with ½ tablespoon of the olive oil and transfer to a baking tray. Bake in the preheated oven for 6–8 minutes until golden and crisp.

3 In a small pan, whisk together the remaining olive oil and the lemon juice. Season and add the chilli and spring onion. Set to one side.

4 Place the eggs in a large saucepan of boiling water and cook for 6 minutes. Plunge the cooked eggs immediately into a bowl of cold water, then remove and carefully peel away the shells.

5 Meanwhile heat the chilli and spring onion dressing very gently until just hot.

6 To serve, toss the rocket and croûtons together and pile on to each serving plate. Place a cooked egg on the top of each pile and carefully cut it open. Spoon over the warm chilli and spring onion dressing, and serve at once.

# ROASTED PARMESAN VEGETABLES WITH EASY-PEASY CHILLI JAM

*These cheesy vegetables make a great starter or canapé, or they can be served as a main-course accompaniment.*

serves 4

1 large bulb of fennel, trimmed and cut into wedges
250g (9 oz) thin asparagus spears, trimmed
2 eggs, beaten
115g (4 oz) Parmesan cheese, grated

FOR THE EASY-PEASY CHILLI JAM:
6 tablespoons bought good-quality tomato or fruit-based chutney
2 fresh red chillies, de-seeded and finely chopped

1  Preheat the oven to 220°C/425°F/Gas Mark 7.

2  Make the chilli jam first. Simply mix the chutney and chillies together. Set aside.

3  Bring a large pan of water to the boil. Add the fennel and boil for 4 minutes. Add the asparagus to the pan and cook for a further minute. Drain the vegetables, rinse under cold water and drain on kitchen paper.

4  Dip the vegetables in the beaten egg and sprinkle over the Parmesan cheese. Spread the coated vegetables out on a non-stick baking tray and bake in the preheated oven for 12–15 minutes until golden. Serve at once with the chilli jam.

 The chilli jam can be served as an accompaniment to plain grilled sausages or pork pies, as an alternative to English mustard.

# CHILLIED FETA AND RATATOUILLE ROLLS

*Great cold for a picnic-style lunch, or you can place the rolls in a hot oven for 4–5 minutes to serve crisp and hot!*

serves 4

1 aubergine, cut into 2.5cm (1 inch) pieces
2 large courgettes, cut into 2.5cm (1 inch) pieces
1 large onion, cut into 8–10 wedges
2 tablespoons olive oil
175g (6 oz) cherry tomatoes, cut into quarters
225g (8 oz) feta cheese, roughly broken into bite-sized pieces
1 tablespoon chilli oil
2 tablespoons roughly chopped fresh flat-leaf parsley,
1 tablespoon roughly chopped fresh mint
4 fresh country-style rolls
1 garlic clove, peeled
black pepper

1 Preheat the oven to 200°C/400°F/Gas Mark 6.

2 Place the aubergine, courgettes and onion on a roasting tray. Drizzle with the olive oil and season with black pepper. Roast in the oven for 40–45 minutes until cooked and lightly charred. Remove from the oven and stir in the cherry tomatoes.

3 Meanwhile, place the feta in a bowl and toss with the chilli oil and herbs. Set to one side.

4 Slice each roll horizontally into three. Rub each slice with the peeled garlic. Take the bottom slice off each roll, and top generously with some roasted vegetables and some chillied feta. Place the next bread layer on each and top again with some vegetables and feta. Place the top on each roll and wrap the rolls tightly in clingfilm. Chill in the fridge for 24 hours and return to room temperature before eating!

# SPAGHETTINI WITH CHILLI, GARLIC AND BASIL

*The very simplest, tastiest pasta dish! If you like a chewier pasta texture, then use good-quality dried spaghetti.*

serves 4

450g (1 lb) fresh spaghettini pasta
25g (1 oz) butter
3 tablespoons olive oil
2 fresh red chillies, de-seeded and finely chopped
1 large garlic clove, crushed
1 bunch of fresh basil leaves
juice of ½ lemon
salt and black pepper

1 Cook the pasta as directed on the packet.

2 In a pan, heat the butter and oil. Add the chillies and garlic and cook for 30 seconds. Throw in the basil leaves and squeeze in the lemon juice.

3 To serve, drain the cooked pasta and toss with the chilli and garlic dressing. Grind over some black pepper and serve at once.

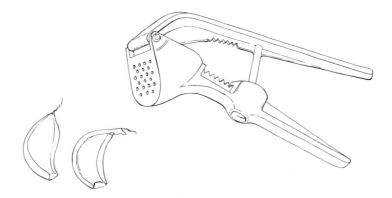

# GREEN BEANS, ARTICHOKES AND SALTED CAYENNE ALMONDS

*The salted cayenne almonds are the jewels on this bean and artichoke salad. Be sure to use whole, unskinned almonds, it's well worth the effort.*

serves 4

100g (3½ oz) unskinned almonds, halved lengthwise
1 teaspoon olive oil
2 teaspoons salt
250g (9 oz) dwarf beans, trimmed and halved lengthwise
200g (7 oz) char-grilled artichokes in olive oil, drained
a squeeze of lemon juice
1 medium bag of salad leaves
½ teaspoon cayenne pepper
extra virgin olive oil

1  Preheat the oven to 200°C/400°F/Gas Mark 6.

2  Toss the almonds in the olive oil, spread out on a baking tray and sprinkle with the salt. Roast in the oven for 10–12 minutes until lightly browned.

3  In a large pan of boiling water, cook the beans for 2 minutes until just tender.

4  Slice each artichoke into two to three bite-sized pieces and transfer to a large bowl. Add the lemon juice and salad leaves, toss together and divide between four serving plates.

5  Top each mound of salad with the hot beans. Toss the toasted almonds with the cayenne and scatter over the salad. Finish with a drizzle of extra virgin olive oil and serve at once.

# CAYENNE CRISP TEMPURA

*If you like dipping sauce with your tempura, try the* Chilli Jam *on page 28 or the* Garlic Tzatziki *on page 131.*

serves 4

450g (1 lb) vegetables (choose from carrot, fine small asparagus,
   cauliflower, fine beans, broccoli)
vegetable oil for deep-frying
55g (2 oz) plain flour
55g (2 oz) cornflour
1 teaspoon paprika
2 teaspoons cayenne pepper
175ml (6 fl oz) chilled fizzy water
1 cos lettuce, finely shredded
1 tablespoon olive oil
1 tablespoon lemon juice
salt and black pepper

1 Wash and prepare the vegetables. Cut the broccoli and cauliflower into small florets. Cut the carrots into sticks and trim the beans and asparagus.

2 Bring a large pan of water to the boil and plunge in the vegetables. Return to the boil, drain and run under cold water until cool. Drain well on kitchen paper.

3 Heat the oil to 190°C/375°F.

4 Sieve the flours, paprika and cayenne into a large bowl. Stir in the water and mix until almost combined, but with a few lumps remaining.

5 Dip each piece of vegetable briefly in the batter and drop into the hot fat. Deep-fry for 30–60 seconds until golden and crisp. Drain on kitchen paper and sprinkle with salt.

6 To serve, toss the cos lettuce with the olive oil and lemon juice and season with lots of freshly ground black pepper. Place a pile on each serving plate, top with a generous helping of hot tempura and serve at once.

# REAL SPICED CHIPS

*These chips are very moreish. Be prepared to make second helpings if your guests are very hungry! Serve as a starter or accompaniment.*

serves 4

900g (2 lb) Maris Piper potatoes, peeled
corn oil for deep-frying
1 teaspoon cayenne pepper
1 tablespoon salt
1 tablespoon smoked or sweet paprika
150ml (5 fl oz) soured cream

1 Cut the potatoes into large, thick chips and soak in a bowl of cold water for 10 minutes. Drain and dry well in a clean tea-towel.

2 Heat the corn oil to a medium heat, about 150°C/300°F. Plunge the chips into the pan and cook for 6–8 minutes until cooked but not coloured. Remove and drain on kitchen paper.

3 Increase the oil heat to high, about 190°C/375°F. In a small bowl toss together the cayenne, salt and paprika.

4 Plunge the chips back into the oil and cook for 2–3 minutes until golden and crisp. Remove, drain on kitchen paper and toss with the salt and spice mix. Serve at once with soured cream for dipping.

 For a different fish and chip supper, serve with salmon fillets or fish cakes.

COOLER THAN **CHILLIES**

# SMOKY PAPRIKA RED RISOTTO

*This recipe can be made with sweet paprika but smoked is now available and gives a great hit of flavour.*

serves 4–6

3 tablespoons virgin olive oil
1 red onion, chopped
1 tablespoon smoked paprika
2 garlic cloves, crushed
400g (14 oz) risotto rice
1 × 400g (14 oz) can of chopped tomatoes in rich tomato juice
300ml (10 fl oz) red wine
approx. 850ml (1 1/2 pints) hot vegetable stock
100g (3 1/2 oz) baby capers, drained and rinsed
175g (6 oz) chèvre goat's cheese, broken into rough chunks
1 bunch of fresh basil leaves
salt and black pepper

1  In a large pan, heat 1 tablespoon of the olive oil. Add the onion and fry for 5–8 minutes until softened and lightly coloured. Add the paprika and garlic and fry for 30 seconds. Stir in the rice and cook for 1 minute.

2  Add the tomatoes, wine and 150ml (5 fl oz) of the stock, and season with salt and pepper. Bring to the boil, then reduce the heat to a simmer. As the stock is absorbed, gradually add more, a ladle at a time, allowing each ladle to be absorbed before adding the next, and stirring frequently until the rice is cooked, about 20 minutes.

3  About 5 minutes before the rice is cooked, stir in the capers.

4  To serve, pile the risotto on to dinner plates or into serving bowls, and scatter the goat's cheese over the top. Finish with a few whole basil leaves and a drizzle of olive oil, and serve at once.

# LEMON AND PAPRIKA HOUMOUS WITH BAKED PIMENTOS

*No need to soak and boil for hours, simply open a can of cooked chickpeas, rinse well, and whizz up for this lighter, chunkier version of traditional houmous. It's great with the whole baked peppers.*

serves 4

4 whole red peppers
3 tablespoons virgin olive oil
2 × 400g (14 oz) cans of chickpeas, drained and rinsed
2 tablespoons hot paprika, dry-roasted
juice of ½ lemon
grated zest of 1 lemon
2 garlic cloves, crushed
3 tablespoons tahina paste
150ml (5 fl oz) hot water
salt and black pepper
1 bunch of fresh flat-leaf parsley, roughly chopped

1   Preheat the oven to 200°C/400°F/Gas Mark 6.

2   Rub the peppers with a little olive oil and place on a baking tray. Bake for 40–45 minutes until cooked and lightly charred.

3   Place the chickpeas, 1 tablespoon of the paprika, the lemon juice and zest, garlic, tahina paste and hot water in a food processor or blender. Season and whizz together.

4   To serve, divide the houmous between four plates and spread out slightly. Sprinkle over the remaining paprika and scatter over the parsley. Sit a cooked pepper on each, and drizzle each serving with some olive oil. Serve with hot bread.

 Serve this houmous as an accompaniment to strips of char-grilled lamb salad in warm pitta breads.

# out of the ground

Bulbs of garlic and lemongrass, and roots of horseradish and ginger are pulled from the ground and popped in the pot to create pungent, spicy dishes in this chapter. Not forgetting the liquorice root which can be cooked up with red cabbage but in my opinion shines far brighter in Sugar and Spice.

# THAI SHIITAKE AND GINGER OMELETTE

*The crispy seaweed is optional in this recipe but gives a delicious crunch with the omelette. Buy it ready-made from the supermarket.*

serves 4

2 tablespoons sunflower oil
250g (9 oz) shiitake mushrooms, roughly sliced
3 tablespoons soy sauce
140g (5 oz) Thai fragrant rice
5cm (2 inch) piece of fresh root ginger, peeled and finely chopped
1 bunch of spring onions, chopped
1 teaspoon caster sugar
5 eggs
1 bunch of fresh coriander leaves
55g (2 oz) ready-made crispy seaweed
salt and black pepper
hoisin sauce to serve

1 In a large non-stick wok, heat 1 tablespoon of the sunflower oil. Add the mushrooms and stir-fry for 3–4 minutes. Stir in the soy sauce and transfer to a bowl. Set to one side and wipe out the wok with kitchen paper.

2 Place the rice, root ginger and spring onions in the wok. Pour in enough cold water to cover and bring to the boil. Reduce the heat and simmer for about 12–15 minutes, until the rice is cooked and the water absorbed, adding a little more cold water during cooking if the pan becomes too dry. Stir in the sugar and mushrooms.

3 Meanwhile, beat the eggs together and add a large handful of the coriander leaves. Preheat the oven and heat the seaweed as directed on the packet.

4 Transfer the cooked rice to a warm bowl. Quickly wash the wok and dry well. Return the wok to the heat and liberally wipe with sunflower oil. When very hot, but not smoking, pour in the beaten eggs and cook for 30 seconds. Swirl the egg mix around the sides of the wok and continue to swirl and cook around the sides of the pan until just set and a large thin omelette is formed.

5   Spoon the mushroom rice into the centre of the omelette and, using a spatula, tip the omelette edges over the mound of rice. Quickly turn the omelette out by inverting it on to a very large serving plate. Scatter over the remaining coriander leaves and a good sprinkling of seaweed. Serve immediately with hoisin sauce and the remaining seaweed.

**(V)** Omit the mushrooms and stir the soy sauce into the cooked rice with 2 duck legs, roasted for 40 minutes, and the skin and meat shredded from the bones.

# TURMERIC SCRAMBLE WITH COURGETTES

*These turmeric scrambled eggs make an unusual brunch dish served on hot buttered toast or muffins.*

## serves 2

25g (1 oz) butter
2 teaspoons turmeric
1 medium courgette, grated
4 eggs
salt and black pepper

1   Melt the butter in a large wok or frying pan. Add the turmeric and fry for 30 seconds. Add the courgettes and stir-fry briskly for 1–2 minutes.

2   Meanwhile, in a bowl, whisk the eggs together, and season well.

3   Add the eggs to the pan and stir continuously until just set.

4   Serve at once on warmed plates with plenty of hot buttered toast.

COOLER THAN **CHILLIES**

# GINGER SUSHI SALAD WITH AVOCADO AND SESAME

*A stylish lunch or supper starter or main-course dish, with the flavours of vegetarian sushi. Japanese pink sushi ginger is available in jars preserved in rice wine vinegar.*

serves 4

225g (8 oz) sushi rice
15g (½ oz) caster sugar
1 teaspoon salt
2 tablespoons rice wine vinegar from the sushi ginger jar
2 tablespoons sushi ginger, finely diced
3 tablespoons grapeseed oil
1½ teaspoons dark soy sauce
2 tablespoons sesame seeds, toasted
black pepper
½ cucumber, halved and de-seeded
1 large ripe avocado, stoned, peeled and thickly sliced

1   Cook the sushi rice as directed on the packet and allow to cool slightly. Stir in the sugar, salt, rice wine vinegar and sushi ginger, and set to one side to become cold.

2   In a bowl, combine the grapeseed oil, soy sauce and sesame seeds. Season with black pepper.

3   Very finely dice three-quarters of the cucumber and stir into the rice mixture. Cut the remaining cucumber into short thin strips and set to one side.

4   To serve, pack the rice into a teacup or large ramekin and turn out a mound on to each serving plate. Top each mound with some cucumber strips and surround with avocado slices. Spoon over the sesame dressing and serve.

# GINGERED NUTS WITH BLACK BEANS AND RICE

*An oriental combination of rice with a black bean, pineapple and cashew sauce. Serve as a nourishing main dish.*

serves 4

280g (10 oz) Thai fragrant rice
1 tablespoon sunflower oil
1 bunch of spring onions, chopped
5cm (2 inch) piece of fresh root ginger, peeled and chopped
4 tablespoons good-quality black bean sauce
juice of 1 large orange
150ml (5 fl oz) water
115g (4 oz) cashew nuts or pine kernels, toasted
2 slices of ripe pineapple, cut into chunks
1 bunch of fresh coriander
salt and black pepper

1  Cook the rice as directed on the packet.

2  Meanwhile, in a pan, heat the oil. Add the spring onions and fry for 2 minutes. Add the ginger and fry for 30 seconds.

3  Stir in the black bean sauce, orange juice and water, and simmer for 6 minutes. Stir in the nuts and pineapple and simmer for another 1–2 minutes until heated through.

4  Pile the cooked rice on to four large serving plates or dishes. Ladle over the sauce, top with a handful of coriander leaves and serve at once.

 Serve with char-grilled chicken breasts.

# DOLCELATTE SALAD WITH GINGER AND APPLE DRESSING

*The very simplest warm salad served with melting dolcelatte and a zappy ginger dressing. Good as a starter or supper dish.*

serves 4

2 thick slices of brown bread, roughly cut into bite-sized pieces

1 large bag of salad leaves

3 tablespoons balsamic vinegar

2 tablespoons olive oil

2.5cm (1 inch) piece of fresh root ginger, peeled and very finely chopped

1 small apple, peeled, cored and finely chopped

2 spring onions, including the green part, finely chopped

170g (6 oz) dolcelatte cheese, cut into bite-sized pieces

1  Preheat the oven to 220°C/425°F/Gas Mark 7.

2  Place the bread on a baking tray and bake in the oven for 5 minutes until golden.

3  Divide the salad leaves between four serving bowls or plates.

4  Place the vinegar, oil, ginger and apple in a small saucepan and heat until very hot. Stir in the spring onion.

5  To serve, sprinkle the hot bread croûtons over the salad leaves and top with the dolcelatte. Drizzle over the hot dressing and eat immediately.

# PAPPARDELLE PASTA WITH LEMONGRASS CREAM AND BROCCOLI

*A rich lemongrass cream dresses this simple pasta supper. Broccoli is a must with this, as it cuts through the richness – and is a great combination.*

serves 4

300ml (10 fl oz) water
2 lemongrass stalks, finely sliced
350g (12 oz) dried pappardelle or tagliatelle pasta
300ml (10 fl oz) double cream
1/2 teaspoon lemon or lime juice
salt and black pepper
1/2 tablespoon olive oil
450g (1 lb) broccoli florets

1 Place the water and lemongrass in a pan. Bring to the boil and simmer until reduced by half. Set to one side for 20 minutes to infuse.

2 Cook the pasta as directed on the packet.

3 Add the cream to the lemongrass infusion. Gently heat and simmer for 5 minutes. Season with the lemon juice, salt and lots of freshly ground black pepper.

4 Meanwhile, in a large frying pan, heat the olive oil. Put in the broccoli florets and fry for 2 minutes. Sprinkle over 3 tablespoons water and cover tightly with a lid. Gently steam-fry for 5 minutes until the broccoli is just tender, adding a little more water if the pan becomes too dry.

5 To serve, drain the pasta and return to the pan. Toss briefly with the lemongrass cream and pile into four serving bowls. Top with the broccoli florets and serve at once.

# AUBERGINE, GINGER AND SESAME TONGUES

*Ginger and sesame blend into a tasty topping for these grilled aubergine slices. Serve as a starter or accompanying vegetable dish.*

serves 4

2 medium aubergines, sliced lengthways into thick tongue-like slices
2 tablespoons dark soy sauce
3 tablespoons sunflower oil
black pepper
1 small onion, chopped
2.5cm (1 inch) piece of fresh root ginger, peeled and very finely chopped
4 tablespoons sesame seeds, toasted
2 tablespoons water

TO SERVE:
1 tablespoon dark soy sauce
2 tablespoons roughly chopped fresh flat-leaf parsley

1   Preheat the grill to a medium setting.

2   In a small bowl, mix together the dark soy sauce and 2 tablespoons of the sunflower oil. Season with black pepper and set to one side.

3   In a saucepan, heat the remaining oil. Add the onion and fry for 5–6 minutes until golden and softened. Add the ginger and fry for 30 seconds. Transfer to a small food processor or blender and add the sesame seeds and water. Whizz together to combine.

4   Lay the aubergine slices on a large baking tray and brush with half the soy sauce and oil mix. Grill for 5 minutes until browned. Turn the slices over, brush with the remaining mix and grill for 5 minutes.

5   Spread the sesame mix over the cooked 'tongues' and return to the grill for a further 4–5 minutes until hot and golden.

6   To serve, lay two 'tongues' on each serving dish and trickle some soy sauce over and around. Scatter with the parsley and serve at once.

# CELERIAC, CARROT AND HORSERADISH REMOULADE

*A light starter for horseradish lovers. When serving, offer thinly sliced brown bread and butter as well.*

serves 4

juice of ½ lemon
½ medium celeriac, peeled and cut into very fine sticks
2 large carrots, peeled and cut into very fine sticks
2 tablespoons mayonnaise
2 tablespoons Greek-style yoghurt
2 tablespoons creamed horseradish
salt and black pepper
1 punnet of cress

1 Bring a large pan of water to the boil and add the lemon juice. Plunge in the celeriac sticks, bring to the boil, drain, run under cold water and drain well.

2 Plunge the carrot sticks into a pan of boiling water, then drain, rinse under cold water and drain well on kitchen paper.

3 In a large bowl, mix together the mayonnaise, yoghurt and creamed horseradish and season well. Add the celeriac and carrot, and combine.

4 Divide the mixture between four ramekins and turn out on to serving plates. Finish with a scattering of cress.

# WASABI NOODLES

*A crunchy wasabi coleslaw heats up noodles dressed with a seedy sauce!*

serves 4

250g (9 oz) medium egg noodles
3 teaspoons wasabi, or to taste
4 tablespoons mayonnaise
1 tablespoon water
350g (12 oz) white cabbage, very finely shredded
1 bunch of spring onions, finely sliced (reserve finely sliced green tops)
2 carrots, peeled and grated
salt and black pepper
1 teaspoon sunflower oil
25g (1 oz) sesame seeds, toasted
15g (½ oz) poppy seeds, toasted

1   In a large pan of boiling water, cook the noodles as directed on the packet. Rinse the cooked noodles under cold water, and drain well.

2   In a small bowl, mix together the wasabi, mayonnaise and water and set to one side. In a large bowl, toss together the cabbage, white spring onion slices and carrots. Add the wasabi mayonnaise, season and toss together.

3   Toss the noodles with the sunflower oil and sesame seeds. Add to the cabbage mixture and toss everything together.

4   To serve, divide the wasabi noodles between four serving bowls, and scatter over the poppy seeds and reserved spring onion tops.

# WARM GALANGAL-DRESSED NOODLES

*Galangal is now fairly widely available. If you can't find it, replace with ordinary fresh root ginger.*

serves 4

4 large carrots, peeled and cut into chunky batons
4 large courgettes, cut into chunky batons
2 teaspoons groundnut oil
1 bunch of spring onions, trimmed
250g (9 oz) rice noodles

FOR THE DRESSING:
5cm (2 inch) piece of fresh galangal (or root ginger), peeled and roughly chopped
1 green chilli, de-seeded and roughly chopped
400ml (14 fl oz) coconut milk
1 kaffir lime leaf
1 bunch of fresh coriander, roughly chopped
salt and black pepper

1 Preheat the oven to 200°C/400°F/Gas Mark 6.

2 Toss the carrots and courgettes together with the oil and spread out on a baking tray. Season and roast in the preheated oven for 35–40 minutes until cooked and slightly charred. About 15 minutes before the end of cooking, add the spring onions.

3 Meanwhile, place the galangal and chilli in a food processor or blender and whizz until finely chopped. Add the coconut milk and whizz again until well combined. Transfer the coconut dressing to a pan and add the kaffir lime leaf. Bring to the boil and simmer for 10 minutes until slightly thickened. Remove the kaffir lime leaf, stir in the coriander and season to taste.

4 Cook the noodles as directed on the packet, drain and toss with the coconut dressing. Divide the dressed noodles between four serving plates or bowls, top each with some roasted vegetables and serve at once.

# HORSERADISH LATKES WITH BEETROOT

*Grated potato cakes, famous from the Jewish tradition, are given a kick of horseradish.*

serves 4

1 large baking potato, peeled, grated and patted dry in a tea-towel
1 large onion, grated
1–2 tablespoons horseradish sauce
25g (1 oz) plain flour
1 egg, beaten
250g (9 oz) cooked beetroot, peeled and roughly chopped
1 bunch of fresh chives, roughly chopped
a squeeze of lemon juice
4 tablespoons olive oil for frying
150ml (5 fl oz) soured cream
salt and black pepper

1   In a large bowl combine the potato, onion, horseradish sauce, flour and egg and season well.

2   In a bowl, combine the beetroot and chives. Season with lemon juice, salt and pepper and set to one side.

3   Heat the olive oil in a frying pan. Using a tablespoon place four mounds of the potato mixture in the pan and cook the latkes for 2–3 minutes on each side until golden brown. Remove, drain on kitchen paper and keep warm whilst cooking another four latkes. You need eight in all.

4   To serve, place two latkes on each plate, top each with a blob of soured cream and finish with a mound of beetroot and chives. Serve at once.

 Replace the beetroot with 225g (8 oz) smoked salmon or pastrami, torn into strips.

# CRUSHED NEW POTATOES WITH TURMERIC CREAM

*Dauphinoise-style potatoes topped with a rich turmeric cream. Great for alfresco eating, with a big onion tart or spinach salad, or anything barbecued.*

serves 4–6

> 900g (2 lb) new potatoes, scrubbed
> 3 teaspoons ground turmeric
> 600ml (1 pint) double cream
> grated zest of 1 lemon
> 1 bunch of fresh flat-leaf parsley, chopped
> salt and black pepper

1 Preheat the oven to 200°C/400°F/Gas Mark 6.

2 Boil the new potatoes in their skins until just tender. Drain well and lay out in a large shallow ovenproof dish. Using the back of a spoon, lightly flatten and 'crush' each potato.

3 Heat a saucepan and add the turmeric. Toast over a low heat for 30 seconds. Add the cream, lemon zest and half of the parsley, and season well. Bring to the boil and simmer for 1 minute.

4 Pour the turmeric cream over the potatoes and transfer to the oven for 35–40 minutes until bubbling hot. Scatter over the remaining parsley and serve at once.

 Good served with griddled fish or roast chicken.

# BAKED GARLIC ONIONS WITH RED WINE GRAVY

*Serve these baked garlic onions with plain mash or* Nutmeg and Cream Cheese Mash *(see page 132) to mop up the delicious gravy.*

serves 4

6 whole garlic cloves, unpeeled and gently bruised
2 medium leeks, cut into 2.5cm (1 inch) rounds
1 large red onion, peeled and cut into wedges
1 large white onion, peeled and cut into wedges
8 shallots, peeled and halved
2 tablespoons olive oil
salt and black pepper
300ml (10 fl oz) red wine
300ml (10 fl oz) vegetable stock
2 tablespoons brown sugar
150ml (5 fl oz) balsamic vinegar
2 teaspoons plain flour mixed with 2 tablespoons cold water

TO SERVE:
*Spiced Mash* of choice (see page 132)

1 Preheat the oven to 220°C/425°F/Gas Mark 7.

2 In a large roasting tin, toss together the garlic, leeks, onions, shallots and olive oil. Season with black pepper, cover with foil and roast for 30 minutes.

3 Place the wine and stock in a saucepan and simmer until reduced by half to 300ml (10 fl oz).

4 After 30 minutes remove the foil from the onions and sprinkle with the sugar. Return to the oven for 20–25 minutes or until lightly charred and golden.

5 Add the balsamic vinegar to the reduced wine and stock, and whisk in the flour and water mix. Simmer gently for 4–5 minutes and season to taste.

6 To serve, top a spoonful of mash with garlic onions and spoon over the rich gravy.

 Try serving the onions with grilled sausages or pork chops.

# ROASTED COURGETTE AND LEMONGRASS SOUP

*Sweet roasted courgettes are brilliant with lemongrass in this summer-style soup. Serve with toasted bought pitta bread, or make your own (see page 140).*

serves 4

900g (2 lb) courgettes, thickly sliced into 2.5cm (1 inch) rounds
2 tablespoons olive oil
900ml (2 pints) water
1 onion, sliced
2 lemongrass stalks, finely sliced
2 tablespoons double cream
salt and black pepper

1 Preheat the oven to 220°C/425°F/Gas Mark 7.

2 Place the courgettes in a roasting tin and toss with the olive oil. Season well and roast in the preheated oven for 40–45 minutes until golden and tender.

3 Meanwhile, place the water, onion and lemongrass in a saucepan. Bring to the boil and simmer for 20–25 minutes.

4 Transfer the cooked courgettes to a food processor or blender and pour in the undrained lemongrass stock. Whizz briefly until not quite smooth and season to taste.

5 To serve, gently reheat the soup and ladle into bowls. Drizzle with a little cream and serve.

# VEGETABLE STEW WITH CASHEW AND GARLIC PICADA

*This rich stew is thickened with a Spanish-style picada sauce to add thickness and flavour.*

serves 4

600ml (1 pint) vegetable stock
150ml (5 fl oz) white wine
225g (8 oz) carrots, thinly sliced
225g (8 oz) sugar-snap peas, trimmed
225g (8 oz) fine green beans, sliced lengthways down the middle
55g (2 oz) cashew nuts, toasted
1 large thick slice of white bread (approx. 85g /3oz), roughly cut into cubes
2 large garlic cloves, crushed
150ml (5 fl oz) olive oil
salt and black pepper

TO SERVE:
1 large bunch of fresh coriander leaves
1 medium bag of salad leaves
cayenne pepper

1 Place the stock and wine in a large saucepan or wok and bring to the boil. Add the carrots and sugar-snap peas, return to the boil and simmer for 2 minutes. Add the beans and cook for 4–5 minutes until just cooked.

2 Meanwhile, place the cashew nuts, bread and garlic in a food processor or blender. Whizz together whilst gradually adding the olive oil. Season with black pepper and whizz together well.

3 Stir the cashew and garlic picada into the hot vegetable stew and season to taste.

4 To serve, toss together the coriander and salad leaves. Divide the picada stew between four serving bowls or plates. Sprinkle a little cayenne over and serve each with a large handful of coriander salad on the side.

# GARLIC, PEPPER AND TOMATO-DRESSED PASTA

*An easy way to dress pasta, using the classic Italian flavours and ingredients you usually find in a tomato and mozzarella salad – but far more satisfying!*

serves 4

350–450g (12–16 oz) dried rigatoni or spaghetti pasta
4 tablespoons olive oil
2 large garlic cloves, crushed
250g (9 oz) cherry tomatoes, cut into quarters
200g (7 oz) mozzarella cheese, drained and diced
1 bunch of fresh basil leaves, roughly torn
black pepper

1  In a large pan of boiling water, cook the pasta as directed on the packet.

2  Meanwhile, gently heat the oil in a pan. Add the garlic and cook over a low heat for 1 minute. Stir in the tomatoes and remove from the heat.

3  To serve, drain the pasta and return to the hot pan. Add the oil, garlic and tomatoes, mozzarella and basil. Season generously with freshly ground black pepper and toss together well. Divide between four warm serving bowls and serve at once.

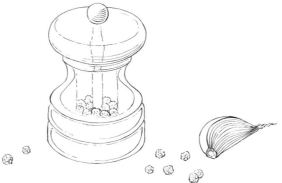

# ROASTED GARLIC SAUCE

*Use this garlicky sauce to dress potatoes or as a dip – but preferably not before a hot date!*

serves 4

> 5 garlic cloves
> 3 tablespoons mayonnaise
> 3 tablespoons Greek-style yoghurt
> 2 tablespoons water
> salt and black pepper

1 Preheat the oven to 220°C/425°F/Gas Mark 7.

2 Roast the garlic in the preheated oven for 15 minutes.

3 Remove the skin from the cooked garlic and place the flesh in a small food processor or blender. Add the remaining ingredients and whizz until smooth. Chill until required.

(V) The sauce makes a lovely dressing for roast chicken sarnies, or a dip for grilled tiger prawns.

# GARLIC MUSHROOMS WITH CHEESE AND CHIVE POLENTA

*You can't beat classic garlic mushrooms, but they are served here with a difference, with a cheese and chive polenta.*

serves 4

4 tablespoons olive oil

3 garlic cloves, crushed

4 very large Portobello mushrooms

1.2 litres (2 pints) hot vegetable stock

225g (8 oz) instant polenta

115g (4 oz) mature Cheddar cheese, grated

1 bunch of fresh chives, chopped

1 tablespoon grainy mustard

salt and black pepper

1   Place the oil and garlic in a pan and gently heat through. Arrange the mushrooms, gills side up, on a baking tray and spoon over the garlic oil. Allow to marinate for 1 hour.

2   Preheat the grill to a medium setting.

3   Place the mushrooms on the baking tray under the grill and cook for 8–10 minutes until tender.

4   Meanwhile, in a large pan, bring the hot stock to the boil. Stir in the polenta and stir for 1 minute or until thickened. Stir in the cheese, three-quarters of the chives and the mustard. Season with salt and plenty of black pepper.

5   To serve, sprinkle the cooked mushrooms with a little salt. Place a mound of polenta on each serving plate and top each with a garlic mushroom. Scatter over a few chives and serve at once.

# GINGERED SOBA NOODLES WITH MUSHROOMS

*Soba noodles – from Japan, and made from buckwheat – are now available dried or fresh in the chiller cabinet. If you can't find either, egg or rice noodles will work very well. Buy the seaweed ready-made in a packet; all you need to do is heat it.*

serves 2

2 tablespoons sunflower oil

175g (6 oz) button mushrooms, finely sliced

5cm (2 inch) piece of fresh root ginger, peeled and finely chopped

2 tablespoons brown sugar

3 tablespoons white wine vinegar

2 tablespoons dark soy sauce

150ml (5 fl oz) vegetable stock

1 heaped teaspoon cornflour mixed with a little cold water

140g (5 oz) soba noodles

25g (1 oz) ready-made crispy seaweed

1 fresh red chilli, de-seeded and finely chopped

1 Heat the oil in a medium saucepan. Add the mushrooms and fry for 5–6 minutes until softened. Add the ginger, sugar, vinegar, soy sauce, vegetable stock, cornflour and water. Bring to the boil and simmer for 5 minutes.

2 Meanwhile cook the soba noodles and seaweed as directed on the packets.

3 To serve, drain the noodles and divide between two large serving plates. Spoon the mushroom sauce over each mound of noodles, then top each with a pile of seaweed and a sprinkling of chilli. Serve at once.

# sowing seeds

Seeds are aromatic. They can be hot like mustard or subtle (therefore used more generously) like coriander. They can be ground, toasted and sprinkled, or made into pastes. Seeds play an important role in all cuisines, from the cool savour of the Scandinavian dill to the perfumed cumin so characteristic of the Middle East.

# TOMATO AND FENNEL STEW WITH GARLIC BREAD

*A simple, heart-warming rustic bake. It's a great store-cupboard dish, but the fennel seeds give it that extra edge, turning it into something special.*

serves 2–3

3 tablespoons virgin olive oil

1 onion, chopped

1 teaspoon fennel seeds

1 bay leaf

a pinch of caster sugar

85g (3 oz) cherry tomatoes, halved

1 × 400g (14 oz) can of chopped tomatoes in rich tomato juice

2 tablespoons balsamic vinegar

salt and black pepper

4 slices ciabatta bread

1 garlic clove, peeled

2 tablespoons roughly torn basil leaves

1 Preheat the oven to 200°C/400°F/Gas Mark 6.

2 In a shallow heat- and ovenproof dish, heat 1 tablespoon of oil. Add the onion, and cook gently for 6–8 minutes or until softened. Stir in the fennel seeds and bay leaf and fry for 1 minute. Stir in the sugar, cherry tomatoes, canned tomatoes and balsamic vinegar. Season well and bring to a simmer, before transferring to the oven for 10 minutes.

3 Meanwhile lay the bread slices on a baking tray and toast in the oven for 6–7 minutes or until golden. Remove and rub the warm croûtes with the peeled garlic clove.

4 To serve, drizzle the garlic croûtes with the remaining olive oil and push at a vertical angle half into the stew, scatter over the basil and serve at once.

**(V)** Omit the garlic bread and serve the stew as a sauce for roasted cod steaks.

# FENNEL AND FENNEL MINESTRONE

*Both types of fennel – bulb and seeds – feature in this chunky minestrone-style dish but without the pasta.*

serves 4

1 large bulb of fennel with herby tops
2 tablespoons olive oil
1 large onion, chopped
200ml (7 fl oz) white wine
450ml (16 fl oz) vegetable stock
450g (1 lb) new potatoes, washed and quartered
2 teaspoons fennel seeds
1 bay leaf
salt and black pepper
2 medium ripe tomatoes, roughly chopped
1 × 400g (14 oz) can of cannellini beans, drained and rinsed
2 tablespoons extra virgin olive oil

1  Preheat the oven to 200°C/400°F/Gas Mark 6.

2  Remove the feathery tops from the fennel bulb and set both to one side.

3  Heat 1 tablespoon of the oil in a saucepan. Add the onion and fry for 5 minutes. Add the wine, stock, potatoes, fennel seeds and bay leaf, and season. Cover and simmer for 25–30 minutes or until the potatoes are just cooked.

4  Meanwhile, cut the fennel bulb into thin wedges and place in a shallow ovenproof dish. Spoon over the remaining olive oil and toss together. Roast in the oven for 20-25 minutes until just tender and golden.

5  Add the tomatoes and beans to the potato saucepan and heat through for 2–3 minutes. Roughly chop the fennel tops.

6  To serve, ladle the minestrone into four deep plates or bowls. Top with the roasted fennel, drizzle over the extra virgin olive oil, scatter over the fennel tops and serve at once.

 Non-vegetarians could add some strips of smoked ham at the last minute.

# INDIAN PASTIES

*Serve these pasties with salad leaves and mango or lime chutney, or try them with the easy spiced* Coconut Gravy *on page 133.*

makes 4

> 1 tablespoon oil
> 1 onion, chopped
> 1 tablespoon ground cumin
> 225g (8 oz) baby spinach leaves
> 1 × 400g (14 oz) can of chickpeas, drained and rinsed
> 375g (13 oz) ready-rolled puff pastry
> 1 egg, beaten
> 1 tablespoon cumin seeds
> salt and black pepper

1   Preheat the oven to 200°C/400°F/Gas Mark 6.

2   In a large pan, heat the oil. Add the onion and fry for 5–6 minutes until golden. Add the ground cumin and spinach and stir-fry for 1 minute until the spinach has wilted. Remove from the heat and stir in the chickpeas. Season and set to one side to cool.

3   Roll out the pastry even more into a large square of about 3mm (⅛ inch) thick. Cut out four rounds about 18cm (7 inches) in diameter.

4   Divide the spinach and chickpea mix between the four circles, leaving a border around the edge. Brush each border with beaten egg and fold over to seal the edges together. Transfer the pasties to a baking tray. Brush each with a little more egg and scatter over the cumin seeds.

5   Bake in the preheated oven for 12–15 minutes until golden and cooked. Serve hot or cold.

# VEGETARIAN SAUSAGES

*These sausages are great served with* Cabbage with Star Anise and Pear *(see page 89) or with the* Easy-peasy Chilli Jam *on page 28.*

makes 8

175g (6 oz) fresh granary breadcrumbs
175g (6 oz) Jarlsberg cheese, grated
4 teaspoons nigella or black onion seeds, dry-roasted
3 eggs
1 bunch of fresh flat-leaf parsley, roughly chopped
black pepper
55g (2 oz) instant polenta
grapeseed oil to shallow-fry

1   Place the breadcrumbs, cheese, nigella seeds, eggs and parsley in a food processor. Season well with black pepper and whizz together briefly.

2   Using your hands, form the mixture into eight sausage shapes. Roll each sausage in the polenta to form a coating.

3   Pour about 3mm (⅛ inch) oil into a large, shallow frying pan and heat until medium hot. Add the sausages and fry for 5 minutes, turning occasionally, until the sausages are golden brown. Drain on kitchen paper and serve at once.

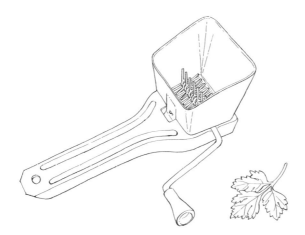

# CHESHIRE CARAWAY RUSTIC ROLLS

*These rustic scone-style wedges are great served warm straight from the oven, with soups, stews, salads and chutney.*

makes 8

225g (8 oz) plain flour
1 tablespoon baking powder
$\frac{1}{2}$ teaspoon salt
black pepper
115g (4 oz) Cheshire cheese, grated
2 teaspoons caraway seeds, dry-roasted
4 spring onions, finely chopped
150ml (5 fl oz) milk
3 tablespoons Greek-style yoghurt

1 Preheat the oven to 220°C/425°F/Gas Mark 7.

2 In a large bowl, sift together the flour, baking powder and salt, and season with black pepper. Add the cheese, caraway seeds and spring onion, and stir to combine.

3 In a jug, combine the milk and yoghurt. Make a well in the centre of the flour mix, and pour in the milk and yoghurt. Mix until everything just comes together to form a soft dough.

4 Transfer to a lightly floured surface and with your hands, gently push out to a rough round about 4cm (1½ inches) thick. Cut randomly and roughly with a knife into eight pieces.

5 Place the dough pieces on a baking tray and bake for 12–15 minutes until golden. Serve at once.

# SWEET POTATO AND CORIANDER SOUP WITH THAI ROUILLE

*The fresh Thai-style rouille and the rich soup make a stunning combination. This is one of my favourite new soups.*

serves 4

25g (1 oz) butter
1 onion, chopped
2 teaspoons ground coriander
675g (1¹/₂lb) sweet potato, peeled and chopped
1.2 litres (2 pints) vegetable stock
black pepper

FOR THE ROUILLE:
55g (2 oz) white bread, crusts removed
1 tablespoon finely chopped garlic
2 teaspoons salt
1 tablespoon whole black peppercorns, lightly dry-roasted
3 tablespoons lime or lemon juice
3 tablespoons groundnut oil
1 large bunch of fresh coriander, including roots and stems, chopped

1  In a large pan, heat the butter. Add the onion and cook for 5 minutes. Stir in the ground coriander and sweet potato and cook for 1 minute. Add the stock and season with black pepper. Bring to the boil and simmer for about 15 minutes until the potato is cooked.

2  Meanwhile, for the rouille, briefly run the bread under cold water and squeeze out well. Place in a food processor or blender with all the remaining ingredients and whizz until blended. Set to one side.

3  To serve, transfer the soup to a food processor or blender and whizz until smooth. Ladle into four soup bowls and top each with a generous spoonful of rouille. Serve at once.

# MUSHROOM FIDGET PIES WITH SOURED CREAM AND CORIANDER

*These open-style pies give a sneak preview of the rich mushroom, Madeira and coriander filling enclosed!*

serves 4

1 tablespoon olive oil
1 large onion, roughly sliced
1 tablespoon coriander seeds, crushed
150g (5$\frac{1}{2}$ oz) baby button mushrooms, wiped
250g (9 oz) chestnut mushrooms, wiped and halved
2 teaspoons plain flour
100ml (3$\frac{1}{2}$ fl oz) Madeira
salt and black pepper
225g (8 oz) shortcrust pastry
1 egg, beaten with 1 tablespoon water, to glaze
2 tablespoons soured cream

1   In a large frying pan or wok, heat the oil. Add the onion and fry for 5–6 minutes until softened and browned.

2   Add the coriander seeds and cook for 30 seconds. Then add both types of mushroom and fry for 8–10 minutes until they begin to soften and release their juices. At first the pan will seem very dry, but do not be tempted to add more oil.

3   Stir in the flour and cook for 1 minute. Add the Madeira, season and bring to the boil. Cook for 2–3 minutes, then remove from the heat.

4   Divide the pan mixture between four ovenproof saucers about 15cm (6 inches) in diameter, and leave to cool. Preheat the oven to 200°C/400°F/Gas Mark 6.

5   On a lightly floured surface, roll out the pastry large enough to cut out four circles, slightly larger than the saucers. Using a sharp knife, cut a cross about 7.5 × 7.5cm (3 × 3 inches) in the centre of each pastry round. Brush the edge of each saucer with egg wash and lay the pastry over the mushrooms, gently sealing the edges. Carefully fold back each cross from the centre to reveal some of the pie filling. Glaze the pastry with egg, and bake the pies in the preheated oven for 20–25 minutes until golden.

6   To serve, place a tablespoon of soured cream on the exposed centre of each pie.

# WARM CORIANDER SEED TATTIE SALAD

*Charlotte potatoes have an excellent texture for this warm tattie salad.
If you can't find them, use new potatoes instead.*

serves 4

1 tablespoon virgin olive oil
1 large onion, chopped
3 tablespoons coriander seeds, crushed
1 fresh red chilli, de-seeded and roughly chopped
200ml (7 fl oz) coconut cream
600ml (1 pint) milk
900g (2 lb) large Charlotte potatoes, halved lengthwise
1 bag of oriental-style salad leaves
1 bunch of fresh coriander, roughly chopped
salt and black pepper

1  In a shallow frying pan or wok, heat the oil. Add the onion and fry for 5–8 minutes until golden. Add the coriander seeds and chilli, and fry for 1 minute.

2  In a jug, mix the coconut cream with half the milk and pour into the pan. Add the potatoes, bring to the boil and season.

3  Reduce the heat, cover and simmer gently for 10–15 minutes. Then remove the lid and simmer for a further 10–15 minutes until the coriander sauce has reduced slightly and coated the potatoes, and the potatoes are cooked. Add a little more milk if the pan becomes too dry.

4  To serve, allow the coriander potatoes to stand for 5–10 minutes. Divide the salad leaves between four serving plates and top with the potatoes. Scatter with the coriander leaves and serve at once.

# BEETROOT AND DILL PATE WITH TANGY CUCUMBER

*A Scandinavian-inspired pâté, which is delicious served with a refreshing cucumber salad and warm, crisp toast.*

serves 4

½ cucumber, peeled, halved and de-seeded, cut into
   3mm (⅛ inch) thin crescents
2 tablespoons fresh chopped dill
3 tablespoons white wine vinegar
2 teaspoons caster sugar
salt and black pepper

FOR THE BEETROOT AND DILL PATE:
450g (1 lb) cooked beetroot, peeled and roughly chopped
a pinch of crushed garlic
55g (2 oz) cream cheese
2 tablespoons dill seeds, crushed

1   Lay the cucumber on a plate and scatter over the chopped dill. In a small bowl mix together the vinegar and sugar. Season with black pepper, pour over the cucumber and set to one side.

2   Place the beetroot, garlic, cream cheese and dill seeds in a food processor. Season and whizz together until well mixed.

3   To serve, mound the beetroot pâté on to four serving plates. Scatter around the tangy cucumber.

# SAVOURY CUMIN CARROT CAKES WITH PEPPERED CREAM CHEESE

*American-style muffins with a sweet cumin flavour. Great served with cheese, soups, stews. It's essentially a savoury carrot cake.*

makes 8

225g (8 oz) plain flour
1/2 teaspoon salt
2 1/2 teaspoons baking powder
2 eggs
2 tablespoons olive oil
2 teaspoons ground cumin, dry-roasted
225ml (8 fl oz) milk
2 medium carrots, grated
225g (8 oz) cream cheese
2 teaspoons cracked black pepper

1  Preheat the oven to 190°C/375°F/Gas Mark 5. Lightly oil eight wells in a deep muffin tin.

2  In a large bowl, sift together the flour, salt, and baking powder. In a separate bowl, beat together the eggs, oil, cumin and milk. Stir in the grated carrot.

3  Quickly fold the wet ingredients into the dry and spoon into the muffin wells. Bake in the oven for 25 minutes until risen and golden.

4  Meanwhile mix the cream cheese with the cracked black pepper and set to one side. Serve the cumin carrot cakes warm with the peppered cheese.

# MUSTARD AND MAPLE BAKED BEANS

*Serve these cowboy-style beans with plenty of crusty brown bread and butter for mopping up!*

serves 4

1 tablespoon sunflower oil
1 large onion, chopped
1 large garlic clove, crushed
2 × 400g (14 oz) cans of pinto beans, drained and rinsed
1 × 400g (14 oz) can of butter beans, drained and rinsed
3 teaspoons dry English mustard powder
1 tablespoon muscovado sugar
2 tablespoons maple syrup
2 tablespoons white wine vinegar
250ml (9 fl oz) dry cider
salt and black pepper

1   Preheat the oven to 190°C/375°F/Gas Mark 5.

2   In a large pan, heat the oil. Add the onion and fry for 5–6 minutes until browned and softened. Add the garlic and fry for 1 minute.

3   Stir in the beans, mustard, sugar, maple syrup and white wine vinegar. Bring to the boil and simmer for 2 minutes. Add the cider, return to the boil and cook for 5 minutes.

4   Transfer the mustard and maple beans to a shallow ovenproof dish, season and bake in the preheated oven for 35–40 minutes, until the juice is reduced and forms a sticky sauce for the beans.

# PINE CAESAR SALAD

*This instant warm salad makes a great fast lunch or light supper.*

serves 4

1 large cos lettuce, torn into bite-sized pieces
1 large ripe avocado, peeled and sliced
4 tablespoons olive oil
2 large ripe dessert pears, sliced
2 teaspoons grainy mustard
juice of ½ lemon
55g (2 oz) pine kernels, toasted
salt and black pepper

1 Arrange the cos lettuce and sliced avocado on four large serving plates.

2 In a large frying pan, heat the olive oil. Add the pears, mustard and lemon juice and briefly heat through.

3 Toss the pine kernels in with the pears, season and immediately spoon over the lettuce and avocado. Serve at once.

Ⓥ Omit the pine kernels and fry 115g (4 oz) bacon lardons in the pan before adding the pears.

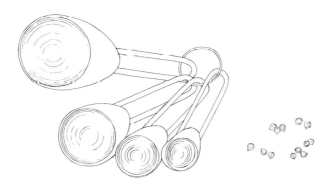

# CRACKED CUMIN TABBOULEH PIE

Garlic Tzatziki *is a must with this cracking pie (see page 131). A crisp green salad is good as well.*

serves 4–6

175g (6 oz) cracked (bulgar) wheat
1 tablespoon cumin seeds, dry-roasted
200g (7 oz) feta cheese, cut into rough cubes
250g (9 oz) cherry tomatoes, halved
1 × 230g (8 oz) jar of mixed olives in olive oil, drained and pitted
1 onion, finely chopped
1 bunch of fresh flat-leaf parsley, roughly chopped
juice of 1 large lemon
3 tablespoons olive oil
black pepper
125g (4$^{1}/_{2}$ oz) filo pastry (approx. 7 small sheets)

1  Preheat the oven to 220°C/425°F/Gas Mark 7.

2  Place the wheat in a large bowl and cover with cold water. Set to one side for 20 minutes.

3  In a large bowl combine the cumin, feta, tomatoes, olives, onion and parsley.

4  Drain the wheat and combine with the cumin and feta mixture. Add the lemon juice and 2 tablespoons of olive oil. Season well with black pepper.

5  Lightly oil a 1.5 litre (2$^{3}/_{4}$ pint) ovenproof glass pudding basin. Brush the first sheet of filo with some oil and lay it over the pudding basin, pushing it gently down to the base and leaving some of the sheet hanging over the edge. This will be used to form a lid at the end. Layer on the remaining sheets of filo pastry, brushed with oil, in a similar fashion.

6  Turn the wheat salad into the lined pudding basin and fold over the excess pastry to form a lid. Bake in the preheated oven for 40–50 minutes until the filo is crisp and golden brown. To serve, turn the pie out and cut into wedges.

# STIR-FRY BROCCOLI WITH MUSTARD AND ORANGE PEPPER DRESSING

*A great way to liven up your broccoli. Serve as an accompaniment to couscous or pasta.*

serves 4

> 1 tablespoon olive oil
> juice of 2 oranges
> 1 large orange pepper, de-seeded and thinly sliced
> 675g (1½ lb) broccoli florets
> 2 tablespoons water
> 1 tablespoon grainy mustard
> black pepper

1 In a large frying pan or wok, heat the oil with the juice of 1 orange and stir-fry the pepper strips for 1 minute.

2 Add the broccoli florets, water and the remaining orange juice. Toss together over the heat, then cover and cook for a further 4–5 minutes until the broccoli is just cooked.

3 Remove the lid and stir in the grainy mustard, adding a little more orange juice or water if the pan looks too dry. Season well with black pepper and serve at once.

Ⓥ Omit the pepper and replace with 2 large chicken breasts, cut into thin strips.

# CUMIN AND AUBERGINE MEZZE PLATE

*Serve this mezze plate with* Instant Pittas *(see page 140) or plain warm pittas for dipping.*

serves 4

2 medium aubergines
1 slice of brown bread
3 garlic cloves, crushed
juice of ½ lemon
2 teaspoons ground cumin, dry-roasted
5 tablespoons olive oil
3 tablespoons Greek-style yoghurt
salt and black pepper
1 bunch of fresh flat-leaf parsley
1 handful of black olives, pitted and quartered

1   Preheat the oven to 200°C/400°F/Gas Mark 6.

2   Prick the aubergines with a fork several times, place on a lightly oiled baking sheet and bake for 35–40 minutes until the skins are wrinkled and the flesh is soft.

3   Soak the bread in a little water and squeeze out. Set to one side.

4   Cut the aubergines in half lengthways and, using a spoon, scoop out the flesh from the skin. In a food processor, purée the aubergine flesh with the garlic, bread, lemon juice, cumin and olive oil until smooth and creamy.

5   Stir in the yoghurt, season to taste and mound on to a serving plate. Scatter with the parsley and black olives, and serve.

 Great as an accompaniment to roast leg of lamb.

# STOCK CHECK PIE

*This is a great and substantial pie, a vegetarian version of a bacon and egg pie. Serve warm or cold, or cut into slices for a picnic!*

serves 6

350g (12 oz) shortcrust pastry
1 tablespoon grainy mustard
1 × 400g (14 oz) can of cooked green lentils, drained and rinsed
115g (4 oz) smoked Cheddar cheese, roughly cubed
black pepper
6 eggs
1 egg, beaten, to glaze

1  Preheat the oven to 200°C/400°F/Gas Mark 6.

2  On a lightly floured surface, roll out two-thirds of the pastry until large enough to line a 23cm (9 inch) flan tin. Fit the pastry into the tin but do not trim the edges.

3  In a large bowl, toss together the mustard, lentils and cheese. Season with black pepper and spoon into the pastry case. Crack the eggs straight into the pie over the lentils, taking care not to break the yolks.

4  On a lightly floured surface, roll out the remaining pastry until large enough to form a lid. Brush the edges of the pie with the beaten egg and lay over the lid. Gently push the edges to seal with the base, then trim any excess pastry. Crimp the pie edges and brush the lid with the beaten egg to glaze.

5  Bake in the oven for 35–40 minutes until golden.

Omit the cheese and add 115g (4 oz) diced smoked bacon, lightly fried.

# popping pods

I think the best-known – and my favourite – of pods is cardamom. Tamarind is now becoming more popular too, with the influence of oriental cuisine, and star anise, the classic Chinese flavour, is also featured in an unusual cabbage recipe. But when it came to vanilla, I have to be honest and say that I threw in the towel.... Vanilla is for me the perfect sweet spice, divine in rice puddings, creamy custards and sticky sugar syrups, so it is not here but in Sugar and Spice.

# CHILLED CARDAMOM MANGO

*Serve this chilled mango as a refreshing starter or as a pudding with Iced Allspice and Coconut Creams (see page 144). Don't be tempted to use freshly squeezed orange juice; a good-quality carton juice from the chiller cabinet will be best.*

serves 4

>  300ml (10 fl oz) carton orange juice
>  10 cardamom pods, crushed (do not discard the husks)
>  2 large, ripe mangoes

1   In a saucepan, heat the orange juice and crushed cardamom pods until just boiling. Remove from the heat and allow to cool.

2   Meanwhile, peel the mangoes and cut into thin slices, discarding the stones. Arrange the slices in a shallow serving dish and pour over the cooled cardamom and orange sauce. Chill for 2–3 hours.

3   To serve, divide the mango between four serving plates and spoon over the cardamom juices.

# CARDAMOM AND OLIVE BAKED RICE

*A very simple dish that's a cross between a pilaff and a risotto. Use long-grain rice and bake it in the oven. What could be easier!*

serves 3–4

> 55g (2 oz) butter
> 1 large onion, chopped
> 225g (8 oz) long-grain rice
> 10 cardamom pods, crushed
> 450ml (16 fl oz) hot vegetable stock
> 1 bay leaf
> salt and black pepper
> 55g (2 oz) Greek black olives, pitted and roughly chopped
> 1 large bunch of fresh flat-leaf parsley, chopped

1 Preheat the oven to 190°C/375°F/Gas Mark 5.

2 In a large oven- and heatproof pan, gently heat the butter. Add the onion and cook for 10 minutes until softened. Stir in the rice and cardamom, and cook gently for 2–3 minutes. Pour in the hot stock, add the bay leaf and season. Bring to the boil, cover the pan and transfer to the oven for 20 minutes, until the liquid is absorbed and the rice cooked.

3 To serve, stir the olives and parsley through the rice and serve at once.

Omit the olives and stir in 115g (4 oz) drained, canned tuna or salmon.

# CARDAMOM AND TOMATO SPAGHETTI EN PAPILLOTE

*A novel way of serving spaghetti, wrapped and baked to give you maximum flavour!*

serves 4

350g (12 oz) dried spaghetti
115g (4 oz) sun-dried tomatoes in oil, drained
500ml (18 fl oz) tomato passata
12 cardamom pods, pods removed and seeds lightly crushed
115g (4 oz) green and black olives, pitted and roughly chopped
salt and black pepper

1   Preheat the oven to 200°C/400°F/Gas Mark 6.

2   In a large pan of boiling water, cook the spaghetti as directed on the packet until almost cooked.

3   Meanwhile, place the sun-dried tomatoes and passata in a food processor and whizz until almost smooth. Transfer to a large bowl, stir in the cardamom and olives, and season. Drain the almost cooked spaghetti and toss with the tomato and olive sauce.

4   Take four large sheets of greaseproof paper about 65 × 55cm (26 × 22 inches). Fold each sheet in half to give a double thickness. Pile the spaghetti on to one half of each of the four greaseproofs. Fold the other half over and twist the edges together to form a tight seal. Transfer to a baking tray and place in the oven for 10–12 minutes until piping hot.

5   To serve, place each pack on its own serving plate and take to the table to open and eat!

**(V)** Fish lovers could drop a handful of scrubbed fresh mussels into each papillote along with a splash of dry white wine.

# LETTUCE AND PEA SOUP WITH CARDAMOM

*Lettuce and peas sit perfectly in this delicate cardamom broth.*
*A brilliant way of using up those outer lettuce leaves that often get*
*chucked in the bin.*

serves 4

850ml (1½ pints) vegetable stock
150ml (5 fl oz) white wine
5 cardamom pods, lightly crushed
1 bay leaf
225g (8 oz) fresh peas
4 spring onions, halved and sliced lengthways
2 slices country-style bread, cubed
1 tablespoon olive oil
1 small garlic clove, crushed
½ cos lettuce, shredded
salt and black pepper

1  Preheat the oven to 200°C/400°F/Gas Mark 6.

2  Place the stock, wine, cardamom and bay leaf in a large pan. Bring to the boil and simmer for 5 minutes. Add the peas, half the spring onion and some salt and pepper, and simmer for a further 5–6 minutes until the peas are just cooked.

3  Meanwhile, toss together the bread cubes, oil and garlic. Bake in the preheated oven for 5–10 minutes until golden.

4  To serve, stir the lettuce into the hot soup and transfer to serving bowls. Top with the garlic croûtons, scatter over the remaining spring onion, grind over a little black pepper and serve at once.

# CARDAMOM-SPICED BUTTERNUT SQUASH

*Butternut squash has a rich sweetness when baked that's even better when enhanced with crushed cardamom. Serve as a generous starter or as a main meal with a simply dressed lentil salad.*

**serves 4**

2 butternut squashes, halved lengthways and seeds scooped out
salt and black pepper
2 teaspoons brown sugar
1 teaspoon cardamom seeds
$1/2$ teaspoon ground cinnamon
40g (1$1/2$ oz) butter, softened

1 Preheat the oven to 200°C/400°F/Gas Mark 6.

2 Season the flesh side of the butternut squash halves with salt and pepper, and place cut side down on a non-stick baking tray. Bake in the oven for about 40 minutes until softened and cooked.

3 Meanwhile in a grinder or pestle and mortar, whizz or pound together the sugar, cardamom seeds and cinnamon. Beat into the softened butter and set to one side.

4 Remove the cooked squash halves from the oven and turn over. Spread the cardamom butter over the surface of the cooked inside and place a large knob in each cavity. Return to the oven for 5 minutes.

5 To serve, spoon some of the melted butter in the cavity over the cooked butternut to lightly glaze, and serve at once.

# TAMARIND, PEAR AND DATE CHUTNEY ON CHEESE ON TOAST

*Cheese on toast with warm tamarind chutney makes a fantastic ploughman's style supper. Just add a glass of beer!*

serves 4

25g (1 oz) butter
1 onion, cut into chunky, wedge-like strips
25g (1 oz) light muscovado sugar
150ml (5 fl oz) beer
2 teaspoons tamarind from a block, or paste
2 ripe dessert pears, cored and thickly sliced
175g (6 oz) fresh dates, roughly chopped
4 very thick slices of white bread
1 × 250g (9 oz) round of Camembert, cut into thin slices
1 bunch of fresh watercress

1  In a large frying pan, heat the butter. Add the onion and cook for 10 minutes over a very low heat until softened. Increase the heat, stir in the sugar and cook for 2–3 minutes until golden.

2  Stir in the beer, tamarind, pears and dates. Cover and cook for 10–12 minutes until the pears and dates have softened. Then remove the lid and cook uncovered for a further 5 minutes until slightly reduced and chutney like.

3  Meanwhile, preheat the grill. Lightly toast the bread on each side and top with some slices of Camembert. Return to the grill for 2–3 minutes or until the cheese is melted and golden.

4  To serve, place each Camembert toast on a serving plate and top with a dollop of chutney. Finish with a handful of watercress on the side and serve at once.

Ⓥ Serve this chutney with any selection of cured meats.

# BUTTERNUT SQUASH, POTATO, TAMARIND AND COCONUT CURRY

*Tamarind can now be purchased in a paste or block to add to curries and chutneys.*

serves 4

1 tablespoon groundnut oil

1 onion, sliced

1 garlic clove, crushed

1 tablespoon caster sugar

450g (1 lb) butternut squash flesh, cut into 4cm (1½ inch) pieces

450g (1 lb) Maris Piper potatoes, peeled and cut into 2.5cm (1 inch) pieces

25g (1 oz) tamarind block

300ml (10 fl oz) hot vegetable stock

1 × 400ml (14 fl oz) can of coconut milk

salt and black pepper

1 bunch of fresh coriander, roughly chopped

1  In a large pan or wok, heat the oil. Add the onion and fry for 5–8 minutes until softened and lightly golden. Add the garlic and fry for a further minute.

2  Stir in the sugar, butternut squash and potato and cook, stirring, for 2 minutes.

3  Dissolve the tamarind in the hot stock and add to the pan with the coconut milk. Season, bring to the boil, and simmer uncovered for 40–45 minutes or until the butternut and potato are cooked, stirring occasionally.

4  Just before serving, stir in the coriander and serve at once with naan breads or plain boiled rice.

# CABBAGE WITH STAR ANISE AND PEAR

*This Chinese-style cabbage with sweet ripe pears is a perfect dish to serve with* Vegetarian Sausages *(see page 64).*

serves 4

150ml (5 fl oz) water
40g (1½ oz) demerara sugar
4 star anise
1 ripe dessert pear, cored, peeled and sliced
675g (1½ lb) Savoy cabbage, finely shredded
salt and black pepper

1  Place the water, sugar and star anise in a large wok or frying pan. Heat gently to dissolve the sugar. Then bring to the boil and cook until reduced by half.

2  Add the pear slices and cabbage to the wok and stir-fry for 2 minutes. Season well. Cover, reduce the heat to medium and cook for a further 2–3 minutes. Serve at once.

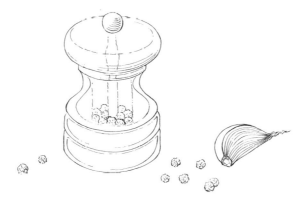

# bush
# berries

Bruised berries and crushed peppercorns are the star spices in this chapter. Once again, due to my personal taste, the allspice berry is to be found in the Sugar and Spice chapter, in a delicious coconut concoction. Back here, appreciate the flavour of ginny juniper without the hangover in *Juniper and Barley Risi* or a rustic *Juniper Cassoulet*. Experience the unusual heat of the Sichuan peppercorn with sweet peppers and tomatoes, or go for it with peppered halloumi cheese.

# BLACK PEPPER PINEAPPLE

*When buying pineapple, making sure it's properly ripe will ensure you can eat the core too. Peppered pineapple is great as an accompaniment to spicy dishes, or with good-quality vanilla ice-cream as a pud!*

serves 4

> 1 medium ripe pineapple, peeled and cut into four thick slices
> 3 tablespoons clear honey
> coarsely ground black pepper

1 Place a griddle pan over a high heat. Lay in the pineapple slices and season with plenty of coarsely ground black pepper. Griddle for 2–3 minutes, turn over, brush each slice liberally with honey and season again with black pepper. Transfer to a serving dish and serve at once.

# MELON WITH PEPPERED PARMESAN

*An unusual yet fantastic combination that I was served on a recent trip to Italy. For a serving variation, see the photograph on page 7.*

serves 6

> 1 orange-fleshed melon (Charentais or Galia), peeled and thinly sliced
> 100g (3$\frac{1}{2}$ oz) rocket leaves
> 225g (8 oz) Parmesan cheese, roughly crumbled
> coarsely ground black pepper
> 3 tablespoons extra virgin olive oil

1 To serve, simply divide the rocket between six serving plates. Top with the slices of melon and scatter over the Parmesan cheese. Generously grind black pepper over each serving, and finish with a drizzle of olive oil.

 Replace half the melon with 115g (4 oz) mortadella.

# CRACKED BLACK PEPPER AND FIGGY BREAD

*Serve this delicious rustic-style loaf with* Chilli Butter *or* Chillied Thyme Cheese *(see pages 133 and 20). Leftover crusts can be enjoyed toasted, with fresh coffee, for breakfast.*

serves 6

675g (1½ lb) strong white flour
2 teaspoons cracked black pepper
2 teaspoons salt
1x 7g (¼ oz) sachet of easy-blend yeast
2 tablespoons olive oil
about 425ml (15 fl oz) warm water
350g (12 oz) dried, ready-to-eat figs, roughly chopped

1  In a large bowl, stir together the flour, pepper, salt and easy-blend yeast. Stir in the olive oil and enough warm water to form a soft dough. Turn out on to a lightly floured surface and knead for 10 minutes until smooth and elastic.

2  Place the dough in a large, lightly oiled bowl. Cover and leave in a warm place for about an hour until doubled in size.

3  Preheat the oven to 200°C/400°F/Gas Mark 6.

4  When the dough has risen, knead it again and incorporate the figs. Shape the dough into an oval and place on a lightly floured baking tray. Using scissors, roughly slash the top of the loaf.

5  Bake in the preheated oven for 45–50 minutes and cool on a wire rack.

# PINK AND GREEN PEPPERED HALLOUMI

*Halloumi cheese is great for griddling. Here it's spiced up with green, pink and black peppercorns, and served on a crisp green parsley salad.*

**serves 4 as a starter, or 2 as a lunch or supper dish**

1½ tablespoons olive oil

2 tablespoons mixed green, pink and black peppercorns, coarsely crushed

250g (9 oz) halloumi cheese, cut into 8 slices

1 large bunch of fresh flat-leaf parsley, stalks removed

a little lemon juice

1 lemon, cut into 4 wedges

1  Heat a griddle or frying pan and wipe over with a little olive oil.

2  Sprinkle the peppercorn mix over each side of the halloumi slices. Place in the pan and cook for 2–3 minutes. Turn over and cook for a further 1–2 minutes.

3  Meanwhile, toss the parsley leaves with the remaining olive oil and a squeeze of lemon juice.

4  To serve, arrange the parsley salad on serving plates and lay over the halloumi slices. Serve each with a lemon wedge and eat immediately!

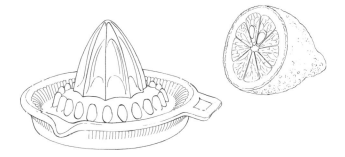

COOLER THAN **CHILLIES**

# SICHUAN RAMIRO PEPPERS

*Ramiro peppers are longer, thinner and sweeter than regular peppers, rather like an extra large chilli, but not as spicy!*

serves 4

4 ramiro peppers
300g (10$\frac{1}{2}$ oz) cherry or baby plum tomatoes
2 tablespoons olive oil
1 tablespoon Sichuan peppercorns, crushed and dry-roasted
100g (3$\frac{1}{2}$ oz) rocket leaves
55g (2 oz) pine kernels, toasted

1 Preheat the oven to 200°C/400°F/Gas Mark 6.

2 Make a slit along the inside of each pepper, taking care to keep the stalk intact, but allowing access to the pepper cavity. Carefully open each pepper slightly and wash out the seeds.

3 Toss the tomatoes with 1 tablespoon of the olive oil and the Sichuan pepper. Stuff the tomatoes carefully into the cavity of the peppers. Transfer to a baking tray and drizzle with the remaining olive oil. Roast in the preheated oven for 40 minutes.

4 Divide the rocket between four plates and top with the roasted peppers. Sprinkle with pine kernels and eat at once with crusty bread.

# MOZZARELLA BREADSTICKS WITH SICHUAN-DRESSED BORLOTTI BEANS

*The Sichuan pepper in these borlotti beans gives an unusual subtle heat. Delicious hot or warm served with thick slices of grilled golden bread and melting mozzarella.*

serves 4

2 × 100g (3½ oz) mozzarella cheese balls, drained
2 × thin sfilatino Italian-style breads
5 tablespoons olive oil
1 small onion, finely chopped
1 garlic clove, crushed
2 teaspoons Sichuan peppercorns, crushed
grated zest and juice of 1 lemon
1 × 400g (14 oz) can of borlotti beans, drained and rinsed
1 bunch of fresh basil leaves, roughly torn
salt and black pepper

1 Cut each ball of mozzarella in half and thickly slice each half into four rough semicircles. Cut each breadstick into ten slices. Take four skewers and thread five bread slices and four pieces of mozzarella alternately on to each skewer, starting and finishing each with a slice of bread. Transfer to a baking tray and set to one side.

2 Preheat the grill to its highest setting.

3 In a pan, heat 1 tablespoon of the oil. Add the onion and gently fry for 4–5 minutes until softened but not coloured. Add the garlic and Sichuan pepper, and gently fry for 1 minute. Stir in the lemon juice and zest, 3 tablespoons more of the olive oil, the borlotti beans and basil, and gently heat through.

4 Drizzle each bread and cheese stick with a little olive oil, and season. Place under the hot grill and grill for 1 minute on each side until the bread is golden and the cheese just beginning to melt.

5 Transfer a stick to each serving plate and serve at once with a spoonful of Sichuan-dressed borlotti beans.

# WARM JUNIPER AND CELERIAC POTATOES

*Juniper and dill give a great flavour to this unusual warm potato salad.*

**serves 4**

1 medium celeriac, peeled and cut into 4cm (1½ inch) chunks
675g (1½ lb) waxy potatoes, peeled and cut into 4cm (1½ inch) chunks
7 juniper berries
300ml (10 fl oz) *crème fraîche*
salt and black pepper
2 tablespoons fresh dill sprigs

1   In a large pan of boiling water, cook the celeriac and potatoes together for 20–25 minutes until just cooked.

2   Meanwhile, using the back of a spoon, squash and crush the juniper berries and place in a small saucepan. Add the *crème fraîche*, bring to the boil and simmer for 2 minutes. Allow to stand.

3   To serve, drain the cooked potato and celeriac and pile into a serving dish. Season the warm juniper cream and spoon over. Scatter with the dill, and serve at once.

 Omit the celeriac and stir 175g (6 oz) roughly broken up smoked trout fillet into the cooked potatoes.

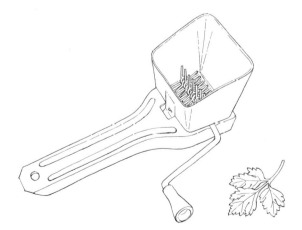

# JUNIPER CASSOULET

*Serve this juniper-infused cassoulet with a crisp green salad.*

serves **6**

2½ tablespoons olive oil
675g (1½ lb) leeks, trimmed
60g (2¼ oz) chicory leaves, roughly broken
8 juniper berries, crushed
4 whole garlic cloves
200ml (7 fl oz) white wine
salt and black pepper
1 × 400g (14 oz) can of borlotti beans, drained and rinsed
1 × 400g (14 oz) can of cannellini beans, drained and rinsed
5 sage leaves
200ml (7 fl oz) double cream
2 thick slices country-style bread, roughly torn into chunks
25g (1 oz) Parmesan cheese, grated

1 Preheat the oven to 200°C/400°F/Gas Mark 6.

2 Place a large shallow ovenproof dish or medium-sized non-stick roasting tin in the oven for 5 minutes until hot. Remove from the oven and add 2 tablespoons of the oil, the leeks, chicory, juniper, garlic cloves and wine. Season well and cover with a lid or foil. Braise in the preheated oven for 35–40 minutes until the leeks and chicory are soft and tender.

3 Scatter the beans and sage leaves over the cooked leeks and chicory and drizzle over the cream. Check the seasoning and return to the oven, uncovered, for 15–20 minutes until bubbling hot.

4 In a bowl, toss the bread chunks with the remaining olive oil and Parmesan cheese. Scatter over the cassoulet and return to the oven for a further 8–10 minutes until the bread is brown and crisp.

Ⓥ Omit the chicory and add 85g (3 oz) bacon lardons.

# JUNIPER AND BARLEY RISI

*Based on the classic Italian rice dish, this recipe is in between a soup and a stew. Rice is replaced with the much underrated pearl barley, and it is infused with the distinct flavour of juniper.*

serves 4

> 225g (8 oz) pearl barley
> 1 tablespoon olive oil
> 1 onion, chopped
> 2 teaspoons juniper berries
> 1 garlic clove, crushed
> 1 bay leaf
> 700ml (1¼ pints) vegetable stock
> 300ml (10 fl oz) white wine
> 225g (8 oz) frozen broad beans, cooked and peeled
> 225g (8 oz) frozen peas
> 55–85g (2–3 oz) Gruyère cheese, cut into slivers

1 Place the barley in a large pan and cover with water. Bring to the boil, cover and simmer for 30 minutes. Drain and rinse well with cold water.

2 In a large pan, heat the oil. Add the onion and fry for 5 minutes until softened. Lightly bruise the juniper berries. Add these to the pan with the garlic and bay leaf and fry for 1 minute.

3 Stir in the drained barley, stock and wine and bring to the boil. Reduce the heat, cover and simmer for 20 minutes or until the barley is just cooked. Stir in the broad beans and peas and simmer for a further 5 minutes until piping hot.

4 To serve, divide between four serving bowls and scatter with the slivers of cheese.

# bark and blossom

Featuring in this chapter are spices that come from trees and flowers. From the stamens of saffron to the flower buds of the clove and the bark of the cinnamon tree, Bark and Blossom contains an array of savoury recipes that can be served as starters or main courses.

# RISOTTO WITH COCONUT MILK AND SAFFRON SPINACH

*A lush, golden risotto served with wilted baby spinach.*

serves 4

1 teaspoon saffron strands
1 tablespoon groundnut oil
1 bunch of spring onions, finely chopped
400g (14 oz) risotto rice
1 kaffir lime leaf
400ml (14 fl oz) coconut milk
1.2 litres (2 pints) hot vegetable stock
15g (½ oz) butter
350g (12 oz) baby spinach
black pepper

1  Put the saffron strands in a bowl and pour 2 tablespoons of boiling water over them. Infuse for half an hour.

2  In a large pan, heat the oil. Add the spring onion and cook for 1–2 minutes. Stir in the rice and cook, stirring, for 1–2 minutes. Stir in the saffron, kaffir lime leaf, coconut milk and 1 ladleful of stock. Bring to the boil, then reduce the heat to a simmer. As the liquid becomes absorbed, gradually add more stock, a ladle at a time, allowing each ladle to be absorbed before adding the next, and stirring frequently until the rice is cooked, about 20 minutes.

3  To serve, heat the butter in a pan. Add the spinach leaves and season with black pepper. Cook for 1–2 minutes until the spinach is just wilted. Serve with the saffron risotto.

 Omit the spinach and serve with lemon and lime grilled chicken.

# SAFFRON POTATO TORTILLA

*Tortillas are great warm cut into wedges, served with a watercress and spinach salad. They are good cold too, and cold wedges make excellent picnic food!*

serves 4

> 1 teaspoon saffron strands
> 2 tablespoons olive oil
> 1 onion, finely sliced
> 450g (1 lb) potatoes, peeled and finely sliced
> 6 eggs
> black pepper
> rock salt

1 Place the saffron strands in a bowl and cover with 2 tablespoons boiling water. Set to one side for about half an hour.

2 In a non-stick frying pan, heat 1 tablespoon of the oil. Add the onion and gently fry until golden and soft. Add the potatoes, cover with a lid and cook until the potatoes are very soft.

3 In a large bowl, beat the eggs and mix in the saffron. Add the cooked potatoes and onions to the eggs, and season with black pepper.

4 In the frying pan, heat the remaining olive oil. Pour the potato and egg mixture into the hot frying pan and, gently shaking the pan, cook for 2 minutes, or until the tortilla is just set.

5 Invert a large baking sheet over the pan and quickly turn out the tortilla. Then gently slide back into the pan and cook for a further 30 seconds to 1 minute on the other side.

6 To serve, turn out immediately on to a serving dish. Sprinkle with rock salt and cut into wedges.

 Serve the tortilla topped with bresaola or serrano ham.

# SAFFRON MAYONNAISE WITH ASPARAGUS

*This mayo recipe makes 300ml (10 fl oz). It keeps well in the fridge for several days and is delicious served with salad, on poached eggs or on top of a baked potato, with watercress.*

**serves 4**

450g (1lb) asparagus
1 tablespoon olive oil
salt and black pepper
4 muffins

FOR THE SAFFRON MAYONNAISE:
1–2 teaspoons saffron strands
2 organic egg yolks
1 large slice of white bread with the crusts removed
300ml (10 fl oz) grapeseed oil
juice of ½ lemon

1 Place the saffron strands in a bowl and cover with 2 tablespoons boiling water. Leave to infuse for half an hour.

2 Preheat the oven to 200°C/400°F/Gas Mark 6. Preheat the grill.

3 Snap off the woody ends of the asparagus and lay the spears on a baking tray. Drizzle over the olive oil and season. Bake in the oven for 8–10 minutes until just cooked.

4 Meanwhile, place the egg yolks in a food processor. Run the bread under cold water and squeeze out. Add to the egg yolks and whizz together. With the processor running, gradually and slowly pour in half the grapeseed oil. When the mayonnaise starts to become very thick, add the saffron with its liquid. With the processor still running, gradually add the remaining oil. Season to taste with lemon juice, salt and pepper.

5 Split the muffins and lightly toast. Lay two muffin halves on each serving plate and top with the asparagus. Spoon saffron mayonnaise over each and serve.

 Replace the asparagus with 4 slices of good-quality cooked ham.

# GNOCCHI ALLA MILANESE

*A semolina-based gnocchi is by far my favourite. Traditionally baked with Parmesan and served mostly with a cooked tomato sauce, try this version using stylish saffron and served with a fresh tomato salad.*

serves 4–6

1 teaspoon saffron strands
1 litre (1³/₄ pints) milk
1¹/₂ teaspoons salt
225g (8 oz) semolina
3 egg yolks
55g (2 oz) Parmesan cheese, freshly grated
salt and black pepper
25g (1 oz) butter, melted

FOR THE SALAD:
6 medium ripe, on the vine tomatoes, roughly diced
1 bunch of fresh basil leaves, torn
1 tablespoon olive oil

1  Place the saffron in a small bowl. Cover with 1 tablespoon boiling water and leave for 15 minutes to infuse.

2  Lightly oil a large dish or roasting tin of about 35 × 25cm (14 × 10 inches).

3  Place the milk in a large pan and bring to the boil. Remove from the heat and add the salt and infused saffron and sprinkle over the semolina. Stir together and return to the heat. Continue to cook over a low heat, stirring frequently for 10–15 minutes. The mixture will become very thick and leave the sides of the pan. Allow to cool slightly, then beat in the egg yolks and 25g (1 oz) of the cheese. Season with black pepper. Transfer to the oiled dish, level the surface and chill for 1¹/₂–2 hours.

4  Preheat the oven to 230°C/450°F/Gas Mark 8.

5  Lightly brush a large shallow ovenproof dish with a little melted butter. Cut the firm semolina evenly into about 15 rectangles, and arrange slightly overlapping in the buttered dish. Brush with the remaining butter and sprinkle with the remaining Parmesan. Bake in the preheated oven for 20–25 minutes until crisp and golden.

6  Meanwhile, place the tomatoes, basil and olive oil in a bowl. Season with salt and pepper and toss together. To serve, place a few pieces of gnocchi on each serving plate and a spoonful of fresh tomato salad to the side. Serve at once.

# SKILLET VEGETABLES WITH A CHEESE AND CINNAMON SAUCE

*Cinnamon is most familiar in dessert dishes, but it gives a gently aromatic and earthy flavour to this tasty roasted vegetable and cheese bake.*

serves 4

250g (9 oz) baby aubergines, cut in half lengthways
2 red onions, each cut into 6 wedges
3 large courgettes, each cut into 3 and in half lengthways
280g (10 oz) baby new potatoes, scrubbed
1 tablespoon olive oil
black pepper
225g (8 oz) cherry tomatoes
300ml (10 fl oz) double cream
85g (3 oz) Gruyère cheese, finely grated
$\frac{1}{2}$ teaspoon ground cinnamon, toasted
2 tablespoons roughly chopped fresh flat-leaf parsley

1 Preheat the oven to 200°C/400°F/Gas Mark 6.

2 Place the aubergines, onions, courgettes and potatoes on a roasting tray and toss with the olive oil. Season with black pepper and roast in the oven for 30 minutes. Add the tomatoes and roast for a further 10–15 minutes until the vegetables are cooked and lightly charred.

3 In a pan, gently heat the cream, then add the cheese and cinnamon and stir until the cheese is just melted.

4 Remove the cooked vegetables from the oven and transfer to a shallow ovenproof dish. Pour over the hot cheese and cinnamon sauce and return to the oven for 10–12 minutes until golden and bubbling. Sprinkle over the parsley and serve at once.

# SPICED APPLE BREAD WITH HONEY BUTTER

*Cinnamon and apples are a classic combination. Serve this bread with the honey butter and mature Cheddar cheese.*

serves 6

225g (8 oz) plain flour
3 teaspoons baking powder
1 teaspoon ground cinnamon
a pinch of freshly grated nutmeg
a pinch of salt
55g (2 oz) unsalted butter
55g (2 oz) muscovado sugar
2 Cox's apples, peeled, cored and finely chopped
approx. 150ml (5 fl oz ) buttermilk

FOR THE HONEY BUTTER:
55g (2 oz) butter, softened
2 teaspoons clear honey

1 Preheat the oven to 200°C/400°F/Gas Mark 6.

2 In a bowl sift together the flour, baking powder, cinnamon, nutmeg and salt. Rub in the butter until like breadcrumbs. Stir in the sugar and apples and enough buttermilk to form a soft dough.

3 Transfer the dough to a lightly greased baking sheet. Using your hands, gently push out to form a round about 2.5cm (1 inch) thick and 15cm (6 inches) in diameter. Mark the dough into six wedges with a knife, taking care not to cut all the way through the dough. Scatter over a little extra flour and bake in the oven for 20 25 minutes until risen and golden.

4 Meanwhile beat together the softened butter and honey, and transfer to a serving pot. Allow the cooked bread to stand for 5 minutes, then break into portions and serve with the honey butter.

# CLOVE-GRILLED MANDARINS WITH STILTON

*You can use ready ground cloves for this recipe, but dry-roasting and coarsely grinding your own gives a prettier look and a better flavour. It's a brilliant warm winter salad with the smell of Christmas! Serve as small individual warm salads, or on one large platter for people to help themselves from.*

serves 4

4 mandarin oranges
$\frac{1}{2}$ teaspoon cloves, dry-roasted and coarsely ground
2 tablespoons caster sugar
a good pinch of salt
85g (3 oz) fresh watercress
55g (2 oz) Stilton cheese, crumbled
1 tablespoon olive oil

1  Preheat the grill to its highest setting.

2  Place the mandarins in a bowl, cover with boiling water, and set to one side for 2–3 minutes. Remove the mandarins with a slotted spoon and peel, removing as much of the white pith as possible. Cut each mandarin horizontally into three.

3  Mix together the cloves, sugar and salt. Place the mandarin slices on the grill pan and scatter over the clove mixture. Place under the grill for 2–3 minutes until warmed and the sugar has melted.

4  To serve, divide the watercress between four serving dishes. Arrange 3 mandarin slices (in a tower if you like) on top of each dish and arrange the Stilton around. Drizzle each dish with a little olive oil and serve at once.

# CINNAMON AND HONEY VEGETABLES ON CITRUS CRACKED WHEAT

*Honey-roasted vegetables served on a mound of soft cracked wheat, flavoured with cinnamon, fruit and nuts.*

serves 4

4 medium carrots, peeled and cut into 4cm (1 1/2 inch) slices on a slant
2 red onions, cut into 6 wedges
2 small sweet potatoes, peeled and cut into 4cm (1 1/2 inch) chunks
2 red peppers, de-seeded and each cut into 6 wedges
2 tablespoons olive oil
2 tablespoons clear honey
salt and black pepper
1 cinnamon stick

FOR THE CRACKED WHEAT:
280g (10 oz) cracked (bulgar) wheat
2 tablespoons virgin olive oil
1 unwaxed lemon, washed and very finely chopped
3 teaspoons ground cumin
2 garlic cloves, crushed

1 Preheat the oven to 200°C/400°F/Gas Mark 6.

2 Place the carrots, onions, potatoes and red peppers in a large roasting tin and toss with the oil and 1 tablespoon of the honey. Season with black pepper and roast in the oven for 35 minutes. Drizzle over the remaining honey and roast for a further 5 minutes until cooked and lightly charred.

3 Soak the wheat in boiling water as directed on the packet. Drain if necessary.

4 In a large pan, heat the oil. Add the chopped lemon and fry for 2 minutes. Add the cumin and garlic and fry for 30 seconds.

5 Stir in the wheat and stir-fry for a further 1–2 minutes. Season well.

6 To serve, pile the wheat on to a shallow serving dish and top with the honeyed vegetables.

# NUTMEG AND ONION BATTER PUDDING

*A puffed and golden Yorkshire pudding style dish, to be served at the table as fast as you can, preferably on crisp dressed salad leaves.*

serves 4

2 large red onions, cut into medium wedges
2 tablespoons olive oil
115g (4 oz) plain flour
2 eggs
300ml (10 fl oz) milk
freshly grated nutmeg
salt and black pepper
40g (1½ oz) Gruyère cheese, grated

1 Preheat the oven to 220°C/425°F/Gas Mark 7.

2 Place the onion wedges and 1 tablespoon oil in a shallow non-stick roasting tin and toss together. Roast in the preheated oven for 20–25 minutes until the onions are tender and lightly tinged brown at the edges.

3 Meanwhile, place the flour in a large bowl and make a well in the centre. Crack in the eggs and gradually whisk into the flour along with the milk to form a smooth batter. Grate in ¼ teaspoon of nutmeg and season well. Set to one side to stand.

4 Add the remaining oil to the cooked onions in the roasting tin and return to the oven for 5 minutes until the oil is hot. Pour in the batter and return to the oven for 16–20 minutes until the batter is almost set and puffed up. Sprinkle over the grated cheese and another ¼ teaspoon of nutmeg, and bake for a further 4–5 minutes until very puffed and golden. Cut the batter pudding into wedges.

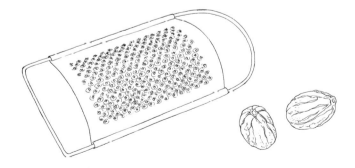

# SAFFRON PASTA PAELLA

*In this recipe, the pasta is cooked 'paella style', absorbing its cooking liquid to give heaps of flavour.*

serves 4

1 large red onion, cut into thin wedges
3 large courgettes, cut into sticks
2 tablespoons olive oil
1 sachet (approx. 0.4g) saffron strands
350g (12 oz) macaroni pasta
700ml (1¼ pints) hot vegetable stock
175g (6 oz) frozen peas
25g (1 oz) Parmesan cheese, freshly grated
salt and black pepper

1   Preheat the oven to 200°C/400°F/Gas Mark 6.

2   Place the onion and courgettes on a large baking tray and toss with the olive oil. Season well and roast in the oven for 35–40 minutes until cooked and lightly charred.

3   Place the saffron in a bowl with 150ml (5 fl oz) boiling water, and set to one side for half an hour.

4   Place the macaroni in a large, shallow frying pan and add the soaked saffron with its liquid and 600ml (1 pint) of the vegetable stock. Bring to the boil, cover and simmer for 12–15 minutes until the macaroni is just cooked, adding extra stock if the pan becomes too dry.

5   Stir in the peas, cover and cook for a further 4–5 minutes until the peas are cooked and the liquid is almost absorbed.

6   Stir in the roasted onions and courgettes and spoon into four serving bowls. Sprinkle each with a little Parmesan and serve at once.

 Omit the peas and replace with raw peeled tiger prawns.

# NUTMEG AND WHITE CHEESE BREAD

*A rich pizza-style bread, accompanied by a crisp, refreshing spinach and radicchio salad.*

serves 4–6

175g (6 oz) self-raising flour
2 teaspoons salt
125ml (4 fl oz) warm water
3 tablespoons virgin olive oil
250g (9 oz) ricotta cheese
3/4 teaspoon freshly grated nutmeg
black pepper
1 heaped teaspoon rock salt

FOR THE SALAD:
1 head of radicchio leaves, roughly torn
115g (4 oz) baby spinach leaves
1 tablespoon extra virgin olive oil
a squeeze of lemon juice

1 Preheat the oven to 220°C/425°F/Gas Mark 7, and lightly grease a baking tray.

2 In a large bowl, mix together the flour and salt. In a jug combine the water and 2 tablespoons of the olive oil. Pour into the bowl and mix to form a soft dough.

3 Turn out on to a lightly floured surface and roll out thinly to form a 30cm (12 inch) rough circle. Transfer to the prepared baking tray. Roughly crumble the ricotta cheese over the surface of the dough and sprinkle over the grated nutmeg. Season with plenty of freshly ground black pepper.

4 Bake in the preheated oven for 15 minutes. Preheat the grill to its highest setting.

5 Remove the bread from the oven and drizzle with the remaining olive oil and sprinkle over the rock salt. Place under the grill for 2–3 minutes until crisp and golden.

6 For the salad, toss together the radicchio, spinach, olive oil and lemon juice. To serve, cut the bread into wedges and serve each wedge with a handful of crisp salad.

# CHEESE AND MACE SOUFFLES WITH CHUNKY FRUIT AND NUT SALAD

*These light soufflés should be rushed straight to the table and eaten at once!*

serves 4

25g (1 oz) butter, plus extra for greasing
25g (1 oz) plain flour
1 teaspoon ground mace
200ml (7 fl oz) milk
85g (3 oz) Double Gloucester cheese, grated
3 medium eggs, separated
salt and black pepper

FOR THE SALAD:
75g (2$\frac{1}{2}$ oz) watercress
1 red apple, chopped
1 celery stick, finely sliced
25g (1 oz) walnut pieces, toasted
1 tablespoon black mustard seeds, toasted
2 teaspoons olive oil
juice of $\frac{1}{2}$ lemon

1 Preheat the oven to 200°C/400°F/Gas Mark 6. Lightly grease four large ramekins with extra butter.

2 In a saucepan, melt the butter. Add the flour and mace and gently cook for 1 minute. Remove the pan from the heat and gradually whisk in the milk until smooth. Return the pan to the heat and stir until the sauce boils and thickens.

3 Remove the pan from the heat and allow to cool slightly, but not completely. Stir in the cheese and egg yolks and season well.

4 In a large bowl, whisk the egg whites until stiff. Carefully fold the whisked whites into the cheese mixture and fill each ramekin two-thirds full.

5 Place on a baking tray and bake in the preheated oven for 12–15 minutes until puffed and golden and just set.

6   Meanwhile, in a bowl, combine all the salad ingredients and season well.

7   To serve, place a small mound of salad on each serving plate. As soon as the soufflés are cooked, place a ramekin directly on each plate and take straight to the table. Eat at once!

# ROASTED PUMPKIN PASTA WITH NUTMEG

*Sweet roasted pumpkin and freshly grated nutmeg make perfect partners for pasta, or try serving them with polenta or gnocchi.*

serves 4

1 medium pumpkin, peeled and cut into rough 4cm (1½ inch) pieces
3 tablespoons olive oil
a handful of fresh sage leaves
280g (10 oz) rigatoni pasta
salt and black pepper
½ teaspoon freshly grated nutmeg
85g (3 oz) Parmesan cheese, coarsely grated

1   Preheat the oven to 200°C/400°F/Gas Mark 6.

2   Place the pumpkin in a large roasting tin with 2 tablespoons of the olive oil and toss together. Roast for 35–40 minutes or until tender and golden. Add the sage to the tin 5 minutes before the end of cooking.

3   Cook the pasta in a large pan of boiling, salted water as per the directions on the packet.

4   Remove the cooked pumpkin from the oven, grate over the nutmeg and drizzle over the remaining olive oil.

5   To serve, drain the pasta, lightly season and toss with the nutmeg pumpkin. Divide between four serving bowls and scatter over the coarsely grated Parmesan. Serve at once.

# mixed spice

This chapter contains two different sorts of recipes. One type consists of ideas for excellent, speedy, off-the-shelf, ready-to-use spice mixes. These instant blends are an excellent alternative, and should not be frowned upon! But if you like to mix and pound, try out the DIY combinations. There are no hard and fast rules! Once mastered, these spicy proportions can be adapted to suit your mood and taste.

# STUFFED FIERY BEEF TOMATOES

*These spicy stuffed tomatoes can be served on toast, or they make a great accompaniment to pasta or cracked wheat.*

## serves 6 as a light supper

3 tablespoons sun-dried tomato paste

3 tablespoons water

1 tablespoon ground cumin

2 tablespoons paprika

2 teaspoons ground coriander

1 tablespoon light brown sugar

6 large beef tomatoes

1 tablespoon virgin olive oil

6 thick slices of rustic country bread

1 medium bag of green salad leaves

1 Preheat the oven to 190°C/375°F/Gas Mark 5.

2 In a bowl, combine the tomato paste, water, cumin, paprika, coriander and sugar.

3 Using a small, sharp knife, cut out an upside down, cone-shaped well in the top (stalk end) of each tomato. Then make a light cut around the equator of each tomato, just breaking the skin.

4 Place the tomatoes in a shallow ovenproof dish and spoon the spiced paste into the centre well of each. Roast in the oven for 40–45 minutes or until the tomatoes are tender.

5 Preheat the grill to its highest setting.

6 To serve, drizzle each slice of bread with a little olive oil and lightly toast until golden. Place each toast on a serving dish and top with some salad leaves. Sit a spicy beef tomato on each and serve at once.

 These tomatoes are good served with pan-fried sirloin steaks.

# CURRIED CAULIFLOWER AND PANEER

*Paneer is an Indian cheese that can be found in the chiller cabinets in your supermarket. Finish the curry with cooling yoghurt and mint and lots of warm naan bread.*

serves 4

1 tablespoon sunflower oil
227g (8 oz) paneer, diced
1 onion, chopped
2 tomatoes, roughly chopped
1 tablespoon turmeric, dry roasted
1½ tablespoons garam masala, dry roasted
2 garlic cloves, crushed
1 small cauliflower, broken into florets
450ml (16 fl oz) vegetable stock
225g (8 oz) frozen peas
4 tablespoons natural yoghurt
1 bunch of fresh mint, roughly chopped
salt and black pepper

1 In a large frying pan, heat the oil. Add the paneer and fry for 2–3 minutes until golden. Using a slotted spoon, remove the paneer from the pan and set to one side.

2 Add the onion to the pan and fry for 5–6 minutes until golden. Place the tomatoes, turmeric, garam masala and garlic in a food processor and whizz together. Spoon into the pan and fry for 30 seconds.

3 Add the cauliflower to the pan and stir-fry for 30 seconds. Pour in the stock, season and simmer for 8–10 minutes until the cauliflower is just tender.

4 Add the peas and return the paneer to the pan. Cover and cook for a further 3–4 minutes to heat through.

5 To serve, spoon into large soup bowls and finish with a dollop of yoghurt and a scattering of mint.

# SPICY FRUIT CHUTNEY WITH CUMIN GOAT'S CHEESE

*Aromatic spices gently simmered with apricots, honey and orange make a simple and spicy, Moroccan-inspired, fruit chutney to accompany hot and seedy, gooey goat's cheese.*

serves 4

2 × 100g (3½ oz) Somerset goat's cheeses
2 tablespoons cumin seeds

FOR THE SPICY FRUIT CHUTNEY:
2 tablespoons olive oil
1 large onion, chopped
½ teaspoon ground ginger
1 teaspoon turmeric
1 teaspoon ground coriander
1 teaspoon ground cinnamon
225g (8 oz) dried pre-soaked apricots, chopped
1 tablespoon clear honey
juice and grated zest of 1 orange
300ml (10 fl oz) vegetable stock
3 tablespoons chopped fresh flat-leaf parsley

1 Preheat the oven to 200°C/400°F/Gas Mark 6.

2 In a wok or frying pan, heat the oil and fry the onion for 5 minutes until softened. Add the spices and gently fry for 30 seconds. Add the apricots, honey, orange juice and zest and vegetable stock. Simmer for 15–20 minutes.

3 Meanwhile, cut each goat's cheese in half and roll each piece in the cumin seeds, pressing the seeds into the cheeses. Transfer to a baking tray, skin side down, and bake in the oven for 8–10 minutes.

4 To serve, stir the parsley through the chutney and serve at once with the hot cumin goat's cheese.

 Serve this chutney with grilled leg of lamb steaks.

# SLASHED JERK POTATOES

*Serve these slashed spicy potatoes with a squeeze of lime and a generous cooling dollop of yoghurt or soured cream.*

serves 4

4 medium sweet potatoes, cut in half lengthways
1 tablespoon olive oil
40g (1½ oz) butter
1 tablespoon Jamaican jerk seasoning
1 lime, cut into wedges
4 tablespoons natural yoghurt or soured cream (optional)

1  Preheat the oven to 200°C/400°F/Gas Mark 6.

2  Using a sharp knife, slash the flesh side of each potato half in a lattice fashion, taking care not to cut right through to the skin. Rub each half with olive oil and bake in the oven, lattice side up, for about 40 minutes until nearly cooked.

3  Meanwhile in a pan, melt the butter. Add the jerk seasoning and gently fry for 1 minute. When the potatoes are nearly cooked, spoon the jerk butter over the latticed flesh of each potato and return to the oven for 10 minutes until golden and cooked.

4  To serve, squeeze over a little lime juice and serve with a dollop of yoghurt if you like.

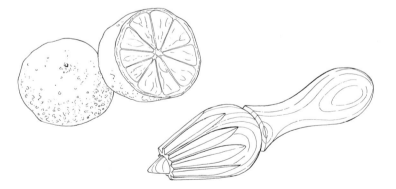

# JERK SPLIT PEAS WITH BUTTERED BLACK RICE

*The black rice used in this recipe is a short to medium grain risotto/ Chinese-style rice. When cooked it lightens to a blacky-purple colour, and is sticky in texture. This rice can be found in specialist food sections and oriental stores, but should not be confused with wild rice (which isn't actually a rice at all!).*

serves 4

> 225g (8 oz) dried green split peas, rinsed
> 225g (8 oz) black rice
> 1 tablespoon olive oil
> 1 onion, finely chopped
> 4 tablespoons Jamaican jerk seasoning
> 850ml (1½ pints) vegetable stock
>
> TO SERVE:
> *Garlic Tzatziki* (see page 131)
> lemon wedges

1  Place the split peas in a large pan of boiling water. Boil rapidly for 10 minutes and drain.

2  Heat a second pan of boiling water and add the rice. Reduce the heat and simmer for 25–30 minutes until cooked.

3  Meanwhile, in a large pan, heat the oil. Add the onion and fry for 5–6 minutes until soft and golden. Add the jerk seasoning and cook for 30 seconds. Stir in the drained peas and 700ml (1¼ pints) of the vegetable stock. Bring to the boil and cook over a medium heat for 25–30 minutes until the peas are cooked but not mushy, adding more stock if the pan becomes too dry.

4  If the rice is cooked and the water absorbed, just before the peas are ready, cover with a clean tea-towel and set to one side for a few minutes until needed.

5  To serve, very gently pull the jerk split peas through the rice. Pile into large teacups and turn a mound out on to each serving plate. Serve at once with lemon wedges and the garlicky cucumber relish.

# MADRAS EGG ROSTI

*Spices, eggs and potatoes have always made a great partnership. In this dish the three combine to make a mouth-watering, substantial supper.*

serves 4

675g (1½ lb) Maris Piper or King Edward potatoes, peeled and grated
2 tablespoons Madras curry powder, dry-roasted
salt and black pepper
3 tablespoons olive oil
4 eggs
½ bunch of spring onions, chopped

1 Preheat the oven to 200°C/400°F/Gas Mark 6.

2 Place the grated potato in a clean tea-towel and wring out as much liquid as possible. Transfer to a large bowl. Add the Madras curry powder, season, and mix together well.

3 In a large, shallow, ovenproof frying pan, heat 2 tablespoons of the oil. Add the grated rösti mix and lightly spread out in the pan. Fry over a medium heat for 7–10 minutes until golden underneath.

4 Using a large plate, turn the rösti out, browned side up. Heat the remaining oil in the pan and slide the rösti back into the pan. Make four indentations in the top and transfer to the preheated oven for 5–6 minutes until browned and just cooked.

5 Crack the eggs into the indentations in the rösti, scatter over the spring onions, and cover with a lid or foil. Return to the oven for a further 5 minutes until the eggs are just set, but the yolks still runny. Serve at once.

COOLER THAN **CHILLIES**

# NUTTY NOODLES WITH WILTED GREENS

*Garam masala and peanut butter make an excellent base for a hot, nutty sauce, here tossed with wok-cooked vegetables and sizzling noodles.*

serves 3–4

1 tablespoon groundnut oil

3 large carrots, peeled and cut into strips

175g (6 oz) cauliflower florets

225g (8 oz) medium egg noodles

175g (6 oz) spring greens, roughly chopped

2 teaspoons sesame oil

FOR THE SAUCE:

1 teaspoon groundnut oil

1 garlic clove, crushed

2 teaspoons garam masala

3 tablespoons crunchy peanut butter

1 tablespoon sun-dried tomato paste

1 tablespoon soy sauce

150ml (5 fl oz) water

black pepper

1 In a large wok, heat the oil and add the carrot and cauliflower. Stir-fry for 1 minute then reduce the heat slightly, cover and cook for 3–4 minutes.

2 Meanwhile, cook the noodles as directed on the packet.

3 For the sauce, in a small saucepan heat the oil. Add the garlic and garam masala and gently fry for 1 minute. Stir in the peanut butter, tomato paste, soy sauce and water. Season with black pepper, bring to the boil and simmer for 2 minutes.

4 Add the spring greens to the wok and stir-fry all together for a further minute.

5 Drain the noodles and toss in the sesame oil. To serve, pile the noodles into shallow bowls and top each with the stir-fried vegetables. Place a large spoonful of the hot sauce on each and toss together. Hand any remaining sauce separately and serve.

 Omit the cauliflower and replace with very thin strips of chicken breast.

# AUBERGINE AND CHICKPEA CURRY

*Like many curries, this dish is excellent when made ahead and reheated. Serve with golden* Turmeric Mash *(see page 132) or warm naan breads.*

serves 4

> 1 × 50g (1 ¾ oz) packet of Italian sun-dried aubergine slices
> 2 Italian sun-dried red peppers
> 2 tablespoons grapeseed oil
> 2 garlic cloves, peeled and roughly chopped
> 1 heaped teaspoon coriander seeds
> 1 heaped teaspoon ground cumin
> ½ teaspoon ground cinnamon
> 1 teaspoon mustard seeds
> ½ teaspoon crushed dried chillies or to taste
> 1 onion, chopped
> 1 × 400g (14 oz) can of chickpeas, drained and rinsed
> 1 × 400g (14 oz) can of chopped tomatoes in rich tomato juice
> salt and black pepper

1 Lay the aubergine slices in a shallow dish. Cover with 300ml (10 fl oz) boiling water and set to one side. In a separate bowl, cover the sun-dried peppers with boiling water and set to one side for 15 minutes.

2 Drain the softened peppers and reserve the liquid. Roughly chop the peppers and transfer to a small food processor or blender. Add the oil, garlic, coriander seeds, cumin, cinnamon, mustard seeds and crushed chillies, and whizz to a smooth paste.

3 Transfer the paste to a large pan and gently fry for 1 minute. Add the onion and gently fry for 2–3 minutes.

4 Drain the aubergine slices and reserve the liquid. Roughly chop the aubergine slices into large pieces. Add the aubergine and chickpeas to the pan and gently fry for 3–4 minutes.

5 Add the tomatoes and strain in the reserved aubergine liquid. Season and bring to the boil. Cover the pan and simmer for 25–30 minutes, adding a little of the reserved pepper juice if the pan becomes too dry. Serve as above.

# TIKKA CUCUMBER

*A hot dressing for cool cucumber. Serve with your favourite vegetable curry or pile on to* Brown Mustard Seed Naan Breads *(see page 141).*

## serves 4 as an accompaniment

1 cucumber, cut in half lengthways and de-seeded
1 tablespoon grapeseed or sunflower oil
2 shallots, finely chopped
2 tablespoons tikka curry paste
200ml (7 fl oz) Greek-style yoghurt
salt and black pepper
$\frac{1}{2}$ lemon

1 Slice the cucumber on the diagonal into very thin slices, and place in a colander to drain well.

2 Meanwhile, in a pan, heat the oil and add the shallots. Fry for 3–4 minutes until just beginning to soften. Add the tikka paste and fry for a further minute. Transfer to a bowl and set to one side to cool.

3 Stir the yoghurt into the cooled tikka mix and just before serving fold in the cucumber slices. Season with salt, pepper and a squeeze of lemon juice, and serve at once.

 Use to liven up cold roast chicken.

# SPICED ROOT VEGETABLES WITH EGGS AND FRESH MANGO JAM

*Healthy 'steamed' eggs with rice and spiced root vegetables. The fresh mango jam is a must!*

serves 4

1 tablespoon grapeseed oil
1 onion, chopped
2 large carrots, peeled and grated
4 small turnips, peeled and grated
2 large parsnips, peeled and grated
2 heaped teaspoons garam masala
150ml (5 fl oz) vegetable stock
225g (8 oz) long-grain rice, freshly cooked as per instructions on the packet
4 small eggs
1/2 bunch of fresh coriander leaves
black pepper

FOR THE FRESH MANGO JAM:
2 tablespoons good-quality mango chutney
1 small banana, cut into chunks
juice of 1/2 lime
1 small ripe mango, peeled and cut into small chunks

1  In a large non-stick wok, heat the oil. Add the onion and fry for 5 minutes. Stir in the grated vegetables and stir-fry for 1 minute. Add 2 tablespoons of water and cover with a tight fitting lid. Reduce the heat and steam-fry for 5 minutes until softened.

2  Uncover the pan, stir in the garam masala and fry for 1 minute. Add the stock and freshly cooked rice and gently heat through.

3  Meanwhile, heat a large non-stick frying pan and wipe out with a little oil. Crack in the eggs, scatter over the coriander leaves and season with black pepper. Cover with a tight fitting lid and cook the eggs for 2–3 minutes until just set.

4  Meanwhile, make the mango jam. Finely chop any large mango chunks in the mango chutney and place the chutney in a bowl. Add the banana and squeeze over the lime juice. Stir in the fresh mango and gently fold together. Set to one side until required.

5 To serve, divide the spiced root vegetable rice between four serving dishes. Top each serving with a coriander egg and serve at once with the fresh mango jam.

 Omit the turnips and stir in 115g (4 oz) smoked flaked mackerel with the rice.

# CRISP HARISSA ROLLS

*Harissa paste is powerful stuff, made from a base of chilli peppers, ground coriander, mint and garlic. It originates from North Africa, and should be used sparingly. Serve these harissa-flavoured rolls with* Garlic Tzatziki *(see page 131).*

**makes approx. 32**

175g (6 oz) filo pastry
2 heaped tablespoons harissa paste
200g (7 oz) cream cheese
25g (1 oz) dried ready-to-eat apricots, finely chopped
4 spring onions, very finely chopped
1 egg, beaten
sesame or poppy seeds for sprinkling

1 Preheat the oven to 190°C/375°F/Gas Mark 5.

2 Heat a small saucepan and add the harissa paste. Gently fry for 2 minutes, remove from the heat and allow to cool slightly.

3 In a bowl, combine the cream cheese, apricots and spring onion and set to one side.

4 To make the rolls, put 2 sheets of filo together and cut into double-layer rectangles about 15 × 10cm (6 × 4 inches) in size. Spread each with a little harissa paste and place a small amount of the cream cheese mix along the bottom, narrowest edge, of each rectangle. Roll each up into a small cylinder shape, and place on a baking tray.

5 Brush the rolls with the beaten egg and sprinkle over the seeds. Bake in the preheated oven for 10–15 minutes until golden and crisp.

# spicy sips and supplements

There is a real mish-mash of ideas here, from a cup of coffee to a glass of beer, from mashed spiced potato to an instant seasoning. Some are accompaniments, some flavourings or toppings, and some are almost complete dishes. But these spiky additions will add zing and zest to the simplest of dishes, giving you a feast of flavour.

# THAI CHILLI PASTE

*Unfortunately, many ready-made Thai pastes are not suitable for vegetarians, so here's a quick recipe for an instant veggie version. This paste will keep for several days in the fridge.*

serves 4

> 1 garlic clove, crushed
> 5cm (2 inches) galangal or root ginger, peeled and chopped
> 1 tablespoon coriander seeds, dry-roasted
> ½ fresh coriander, with the root on if possible, washed
> 1 teaspoon salt
> 2 red chillies, de-seeded and chopped
> 2 kaffir lime leaves, shredded
> 2 tablespoons vegetable oil

1 Place all the ingredients in a small food processor or pestle and mortar and whizz or pound until smooth.

2 To use, fry for 1-2 minutes in a wok, and stir into soups, stews or coconut milk, or toss with buttered noodles, potatoes or pasta.

# GARLIC TZATZIKI

*Serve as a refreshing dip or cold sauce, or pull through plain mashed potato, or pop on top of a baked ordinary or sweet potato.*

serves 4

> 200g (7 oz) Greek-style yoghurt
> 2 tablespoons roughly chopped fresh mint
> 1 tablespoon olive oil
> 1 fat garlic clove, crushed
> 2 tablespoons water
> salt and black pepper

1 Simply place all the ingredients in a bowl. Mix together and season to taste.

# SPICED MASH

*Here are four ways of spicing up your basic mashed potato, and giving it a bit of a kick! First of all cook 900g (2 lb) peeled potatoes in salted water until tender, then mash with 150ml (5 fl oz) boiling milk.*

serves 4

## TURMERIC MASH

Fry a chopped bunch of spring onions in 40g (1½ oz) butter and fry for 3-4 minutes. Add 2 heaped teaspoons of turmeric and fry for a further 30 seconds. Combine with the hot mashed potato.

## HORSERADISH MASH

Simply stir 4 tablespoons creamed horseradish into your mash or, for an even bigger kick, buy some ready-made wasabi paste and add to taste!

## NUTMEG AND CREAM CHEESE MASH

Mash the potatoes with ½ teaspoon freshly grated nutmeg and 100g (3½ oz) cream cheese, seasoning to taste.

## MUSTARD, HONEY AND BUTTER MASH

In a small bowl, combine 4 tablespoons grainy mustard, 2 tablespoons clear honey and 55g (2 oz) melted butter. Stir into the mash and serve at once.

# COCONUT GRAVY

*Serve this speedy coconut gravy with roasted vegetables, spooned over mash or with* Indian Pasties *(see page 63).*

serves 4-6

> 2 tablespoons Madras curry paste
> 1 tablespoon tomato purée
> 1 × 400ml (14 fl oz) can of coconut milk
> a squeeze of lemon juice

1 Heat a medium saucepan. Add the curry paste and tomato purée and fry for 30 seconds.

2 Add the coconut milk and simmer for 5 minutes. Finish with a squeeze of lemon juice and serve.

(V) Try this gravy served with fillets of cod or haddock.

# CHILLI BUTTER

*Chilli butter is delicious tossed through steamed vegetables, pasta, couscous or rice, as a topping for baked sweet potatoes or corn on the cob, or it can just be enjoyed with warm crusty bread! Store the butter in the fridge, but allow to come to room temperature before serving.*

serves 4

> 115g (4 oz) slightly salted butter, softened
> 1 red chilli, de-seeded and finely chopped
> 1 green chilli, de-seeded and finely chopped

1 Simply combine the butter and chopped chillies and transfer to a small serving dish.

(V) Try topping griddled rump steak or fish with a knob of chilli butter.

# INSTANT SPICY 'DRESSINGS'

*The following instant dressings and seasonings are great ways to spice up 350-450g (12-16 oz) of rice, cracked wheat or couscous, to serve four to six people. Quick to make, simply stir them through the hot grain (or pasta) and serve at once!*

## LEMON, PARSLEY AND GARLIC GREMOLATA DRESSING

*To dress cooked cracked wheat, couscous, pasta or long-grain or brown rice.*

grated zest of 1 lemon
juice of ¹/₂ lemon
2 garlic cloves, crushed
2 tablespoons olive oil
1 large bunch of fresh flat-leaf parsley
salt and black pepper

1 Simply combine all the ingredients together in a large bowl and season well. Stir in your chosen grain, and serve at once.

## CUMIN, ORANGE AND GARLIC DRESSING

*To dress cracked wheat or couscous.*

¹/₂ orange, roughly chopped
1 garlic clove, crushed
2 tablespoons ground cumin, dry-roasted
salt and black pepper

1 Place all the ingredients in a small food processor or blender and whizz until the orange is finely chopped. Season, stir in your chosen grain, and serve at once.

## SEEDY SEASONING

*To dress cooked cracked wheat or couscous.*

2 tablespoons sunflower seeds, toasted
2 tablespoons pumpkin seeds, toasted
2 tablespoons poppy seeds, dry-roasted
2 tablespoons sesame seeds, dry-roasted
1/2 teaspoon caster sugar
1/2 teaspoon salt

1 Combine all the warm seeds together with the sugar and salt. Pull through your chosen grain and serve at once.

## CHILLI, COCONUT AND LIME THAI SEASONING

*To dress cooked basmati, long-grain or sticky Thai rice.*

2 teaspoons dried chilli flakes
1 tablespoon boiling water
zest and juice of 1 lime
2 tablespoons unsweetened desiccated coconut,
    dry-roasted until golden
salt and black pepper

1 Place the chilli in a small dish and pour over the boiling water. Set to one side for 5 minutes.

2 Stir in the lime zest and juice and toasted coconut, add to your chosen rice and season to taste. Serve at once.

# GARLIC, CHILLI, CASHEW AND CORIANDER SEASONING

*To dress cooked basmati, long-grain or sticky Thai rice.*

100g (3½ oz) cashew nuts, toasted and roughly chopped
1 large fresh red chilli, de-seeded and finely chopped
1 garlic clove, crushed
1 large bunch of fresh coriander leaves, roughly chopped
salt and black pepper

1  In a bowl, combine all the ingredients together. Stir in your chosen rice and lightly season. Serve at once.


# ROASTED RED ONION AND GARLIC DRESSING

*To dress cooked pasta or couscous.*

4 large red onions, peeled and each cut into 8 wedges
8 garlic cloves
3 tablespoons olive oil
4 tablespoons balsamic vinegar
1 bunch of fresh mint, roughly chopped
salt and black pepper

1  Preheat the oven to 200°C/400°F/Gas Mark 6.

2  Place the onions and garlic in a roasting tin and drizzle with 2 tablespoons of the olive oil. Season and roast in the oven for 25 minutes. Spoon over the vinegar and return to the oven for a further 10 minutes.

3  To serve, toss the roasted onions and garlic with the mint and your chosen pasta or couscous. Season to taste with salt and pepper and drizzle with the remaining oil. Serve at once, allowing each person to squeeze the pulp from the garlic cloves over their serving to taste.

# AVOCADO RELISH

*This zingy relish is great with Vegetarian Sausages (see page 64), stirred through pasta, or simply served open-sandwich-style on lightly buttered rye bread, with a few coriander leaves sprinkled on top.*

serves 4

> 1 large ripe avocado, stoned, peeled and very finely diced
> juice of ½ lemon
> 115g (4 oz) cherry tomatoes, diced
> 1 tablespoon finely chopped onion
> 1 tablespoon olive oil
> 2 tablespoons roughly chopped fresh coriander leaves
> 2 teaspoons good-quality tomato chutney
> 1 fresh red chilli, de-seeded and finely chopped
> salt and black pepper

1  Place the diced avocado in a bowl and squeeze over the lemon juice.

2  Add all the remaining ingredients to the bowl, mix gently together and season with a little salt and lots of freshly ground black pepper.

 Serve as a delicious relish for spicy beef or chicken burgers.

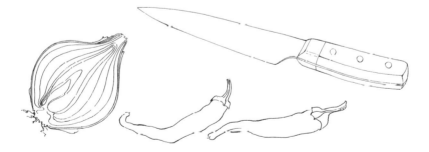

# HOT GINGERED ALE

*Serve this gingered warming ale to keep out the winter chills, great after a nippy walk home, or when you've been carol-singing!*

serves 4

600ml (1 pint) pale ale
2 generous tablespoons of clear honey, or to taste
150ml (5 fl oz) ginger wine

1  Place the beer and honey in a large pan and gently heat until just boiling. Stir in the ginger wine.

2  Pour the hot gingered ale into four teacups or small glasses and serve at once.

# SWEET CARDAMOM COFFEE AND CREAM

*Transport yourself back to the 1970s with this spiced version of a sweet after-dinner coffee which can double as a pud. Place a teaspoon in each glass before pouring in the hot coffee to prevent cracking.*

serves 4

3–4 tablespoons good-quality ground cafetière coffee
6 cardamom pods, crushed
8 teaspoons brown sugar
300ml (10 fl oz) double cream, very lightly whipped

1  Place the coffee and cardamom pods in a medium cafetière and pour over the boiling water. Stir once and allow to stand for 5 minutes before plunging.

2  Place 2 teaspoons of sugar in each serving glass, then pour in the cardamom coffee. Carefully spoon on some double cream and serve at once.

# INSTANT PITTAS

*Jazz up plain pitta breads and use as an accompaniment to soups and stews.*

serves 4

4 pitta breads
25g (1 oz) butter
1 tablespoon virgin olive oil
½ teaspoon mixed dried green, pink and black peppercorns,
 coarsely ground
1 bunch of fresh basil leaves, shredded

1 Preheat the grill.

2 Using a sharp knife, make five diagonal cuts across one side of each pitta bread, taking care not to cut all the way through. Place on a tray and grill until lightly golden.

3 In a pan, melt the butter and add the olive oil, peppercorns and basil. Heat briefly until the basil becomes bright green.

4 Brush the warm pittas with the aromatic butter and eat immediately.

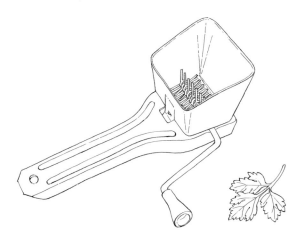

# BROWN MUSTARD SEED NAAN BREAD

*A quick and easy grilled naan bread recipe, made without yeast.*
*Serve with any curry.*

makes 4

> 225g (8 oz) self-raising flour
> 2 tablespoons brown mustard seeds, dry-roasted
> 1 teaspoon salt
> black pepper
> 150g (5 oz) natural yoghurt
> 25g (1 oz) butter

1 Preheat the grill to a medium setting.

2 Place the flour in a bowl and mix in the mustard seeds, salt and plenty of black pepper. Stir in the yoghurt and mix well to form a soft dough.

3 Divide the dough into four and, using your hands, press out each piece into a rough oval about 5mm (1/4 inch) thick.

4 Transfer to a non-stick baking tray dusted with a little flour, and grill for about 3 minutes on each side until puffed and golden.

5 Brush each immediately with a little butter and serve at once.

# sugar and spice

Warm and aromatic, or fresh and hot, sugar and spice make a brilliant combination. From the classic pudding spices of cinnamon, vanilla, nutmeg and ginger to the more unusual flavours of liquorice, lemongrass and red chilli, spices play an important role at every stage of the meal – even here, at the pudding stage!

# CHOCOLATE AND VANILLA PRUNE BAKED TART

*The most amazing combination for the ultimate chocolate tart! If you are lucky enough to be able to find vanilla-flavoured prunes, they will not need to be soaked overnight with vanilla extract.*

## serves 8–10

250g (9 oz) ready-to-eat prunes
4 tablespoons boiling water
3 teaspoons vanilla extract
375g (13 oz) bought shortcrust pastry
100g (3½ oz) bitter continental chocolate
150ml (5 fl oz) double cream
250g (9 oz) mascarpone cheese
2 eggs, beaten

1 Place the prunes in a bowl with the boiling water and vanilla extract and leave to soak overnight.

2 Preheat the oven to 200°C/400°F/Gas Mark 6.

3 On a lightly floured surface, roll out the pastry and use to line a 30cm (12 inch) loose-bottomed tart tin. Chill for 15 minutes.

4 Line the pastry tart case with greaseproof paper and fill with baking beans. Bake in the oven for 10–15 minutes. Remove the paper and beans and return the tart case to the oven for 3–5 minutes until it is just cooked. Remove from the oven and reduce the heat to 180°C/350°F/Gas Mark 4.

5 Place the chocolate and cream in a bowl over a pan of simmering water until the chocolate has just melted. Remove from the heat and add the mascarpone and beaten eggs. Cut the prunes in half and stir into the chocolate mixture with any soaking juices.

6 Pour the chocolate and prune mix into the cooked tart case and return to the oven for 20–25 minutes or until just set. (The top is supposed to crack!)

7 Serve at room temperature or chilled.

# ICED ALLSPICE AND COCONUT CREAMS

*These iced creams are also great served with* Chilled Cardamom Mango *(see page 80).*

serves 4

> 250g (9 oz) mascarpone cheese
> 300ml (10 fl oz) coconut cream
> 1 tablespoon caster sugar or to taste
> grated zest of 2 limes
> 1 teaspoon ground allspice, dry-roasted
> fresh raspberries to serve

1 Place the mascarpone in a large bowl and gradually whisk in the coconut cream, sugar, lime zest and allspice until smooth.

2 Pour into four ramekins or small teacups and place in the freezer for about 1 hour, or until just set.

3 To serve, turn out the iced creams and serve with the fresh raspberries.


# RHUBARB AND CARDAMOM PUD

*Serve this truly scrumptious rhubarb pud with easy* Liquorice Custard *or* Cantaloupe and Ginger Sauce *(see page 153).*

serves 6–8

> 1 small unwaxed lemon, roughly chopped
> 175g (6 oz) unsalted butter
> 175g (6 oz) caster sugar
> 10 cardamom pods, husks removed
> 2 eggs
> 85g (3 oz) instant polenta
> 100g (3½ oz) ground almonds
> 1 teaspoon baking powder
> 280g (10 oz) rhubarb, cut into 7.5cm (3 inch) thin sticks

1 Preheat the oven to 190°C/375°F/Gas Mark 5. Lightly oil a 23cm (9 inch) non-stick springform or sponge tin, and line the edges with greaseproof paper.

2 In a food processor, blend the lemon until very finely chopped. Add the butter and 115g (4 oz) sugar and whizz again.

3 Crush the cardamom seeds with the remaining sugar. Add to the food processor along with the eggs and whizz again. Finally mix the polenta, ground almonds and baking powder, add to the processor and whizz to combine.

4 Spoon the mixture into the prepared cake tin and lay the rhubarb sticks on the surface like the spokes of a wheel. Sprinkle with a little extra caster sugar and bake in the oven for about 1 hour until firm and golden.

5 Allow to stand for 20 minutes, then serve as suggested.

# ORANGE AND CINNAMON COOKIES

*These speedy biscuits are excellent served with fruit puddings or ice-cream. You can also dip them in melted plain chocolate, then allow the chocolate to harden, to be served with coffee as a petit-four.*

makes 10

> 115g (4 oz) butter
> 55g (2 oz) brown sugar
> grated rind of 1 orange
> 140g (5 oz) self-raising flour
> 3 teaspoons ground cinnamon
> icing sugar for dusting

1 Preheat the oven to 190°C/375°F/Gas Mark 5. Lightly flour a baking tray.

2 In a mixing bowl cream together the butter, sugar and orange rind. Sift in the flour and cinnamon, and mix well.

3 Divide the mixture into ten and roll with your hands into rounds. Place on the floured baking tray. Flatten the cookies with a wet fork.

4 Bake in the preheated oven for 10–15 minutes. Allow to cool slightly before transferring to a wire rack. Dust with icing sugar and serve warm or cold.

# NUTMEG AND BANANA TOFFEE TART

*A bubbling hot, upside-down banana, toffee and nutmeg extravaganza!*

serves 6

85g (3 oz) unsalted butter
85g (3 oz) muscovado sugar
8 medium bananas, peeled
375g (13 oz) ready-rolled puff pastry
1/2–1 teaspoon freshly grated nutmeg
single cream to serve (optional)

1 Preheat the oven to 200°C/400°F/Gas Mark 6.

2 In a pan, melt the butter and sugar together and simmer for 2–3 minutes until well dissolved and bubbling hot. Pour half of this mixture into the base of a 25cm (10 inch) sponge tin or round ovenproof dish.

3 Arrange six of the bananas down the centre of the tin and lay the remaining two down each side. Pour the remaining butter and sugar mixture over the bananas.

4 On a lightly floured surface, roll out the pastry a little bit thinner to form a square. Using a sharp knife, cut out a circle, slightly larger than the tin. Lift the pastry over the bananas like a blanket and lightly tuck the edges in. Cut a 2.5cm (1 inch) slash in the pastry.

5 Bake in the preheated oven for about 20 minutes until bubbling hot and the puff pastry is golden and cooked.

6 To serve, remove from the oven and leave to stand for 3–4 minutes before carefully turning out on to a large serving plate with the bananas facing up. Generously grate with the nutmeg and serve at once with single cream if desired.

# PLUM GALETTE

*A plum and cinnamon sweet-style pizza. Delicious when served with hunks of cheese, especially goat's cheese or Stilton.*

serves 6–8

900g (2 lb) mixed plums, stoned and quartered
85g (3 oz) unsalted butter
115g (4 oz) soft brown sugar
2 teaspoons ground cinnamon
juice of 2 oranges
1 punnet of blackberries or red berries (optional)
icing sugar to decorate

FOR THE BREAD DOUGH:
350g (12 oz ) strong white flour
$\frac{1}{2}$ teaspoon salt
3.5g ($\frac{1}{2}$ sachet) easy-blend yeast
1 egg, beaten
15g ($\frac{1}{2}$ oz) butter, melted
200ml (7 fl oz) warm milk
grated rind of 2 lemons
grated rind of 2 oranges

1 To make the bread dough, in a large bowl, stir together the flour, salt and easy-blend yeast. Stir in the egg, melted butter and enough warm milk to form a soft dough. Turn out on to a lightly floured surface and knead for 20 minutes until smooth and elastic.

2 Place the dough in a lightly oiled, large bowl. Cover and leave in a warm place for about 1 hour until doubled in size.

3 Preheat the oven to 200°C/400°F/Gas Mark 6. Lightly grease a 35cm (14 inch) loose-bottomed flan ring or a large baking tray.

4 On a lightly floured surface, knock back the dough and knead in the grated lemon and orange rinds. Roll the dough out into a rough round and place in the prepared tin or tray.

5 Scatter the plums over the dough and dot over the butter. Mix the brown sugar and cinnamon together and sprinkle over the plums. Pour over the orange juice.

6   Bake in the preheated oven for 35–40 minutes or until the dough is cooked and the plums bubbling hot.

7   To serve, place on a scrubbed wooden chopping board, scatter over the berries and lightly dust with icing sugar.

# CITRUS FRUIT SOUP

*Serve baby meringues, warm shortbread or* Orange and Cinnamon Cookies *(see page 145) with this warming winter dessert.*

serves 4

> 10 seedless satsumas
> 850ml (1 1/2 pints) orange juice
> 25g (1 oz) unsalted butter
> grated zest of 1 orange
> 25g (1 oz) sugar
> 2 star anise or 2 cloves
> 1 bay leaf
> 1/2 teaspoon ground cinnamon
> 3 tablespoons Grand Marnier
> 1 bunch of fresh mint leaves
> 4 tablespoons *crème fraîche*

1   Place the satsumas in a large heatproof bowl and cover with boiling water. Leave for 4–5 minutes, drain, then remove the peel and pith. Cut some of the whole satsumas in half, horizontally.

2   Place the orange juice, butter, orange zest, sugar and spices in a pan. Bring to the boil and simmer for 8 minutes. Add the satsumas and simmer gently for 2–3 minutes, whilst spooning over the syrup.

3   To serve, heat the Grand Marnier, ignite and pour over the satsumas. Ladle into four serving bowls and top with mint leaves and *crème fraîche*.

# GINGER AND LIME BAKED CUSTARDS WITH PASSIONFRUIT

*These simple baked custards make use of the excellent stem ginger cookies or biscuits now available in supermarkets. For a practical serving idea, make the custards in teacups, and place them on their saucers before serving.*

serves 4

>   300ml (10 fl oz) double cream
>   200ml (7 fl oz) milk
>   3 eggs, beaten
>   1 tablespoon caster sugar
>   grated zest of 1 lime
>   4 stem ginger cookies, roughly broken up into chunks
>   4 passionfruit, scooped out

1   Preheat the oven to 220°C/425°F/Gas Mark 7.

2   In a large bowl, mix together the cream, milk, eggs, sugar, lime zest and cookie chunks. Pour into four large ramekins or teacups.

3   Place the ramekins in a baking dish and pour in enough hot water to come halfway up their sides. Place this bain-marie in the oven for about 25 minutes or until the custards are just set.

4   Serve each baked custard topped with a spoonful of passionfruit flesh and seeds.

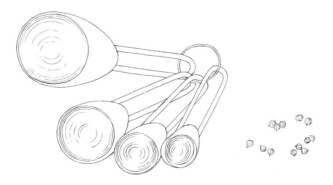

# GINGER FRESH FRUITS WITH APRICOT SMOOTHIE

*A modern version of posh, plated fruit salad with a tangy ginger and apricot smoothie.*

serves 4

1 small ripe Galia melon, de-seeded, peeled and cut into thick
   wedge-like slices
3 kiwi fruit, peeled and cut lengthways into wedges
225g (8 oz) green grapes
5 pieces stem ginger in syrup, drained and finely chopped

FOR THE APRICOT SMOOTHIE:
450g (1 lb) apricots, stoned
4 tablespoons stem ginger syrup (from the jar)
150ml (5 fl oz) water

1  Place the apricots, stem ginger syrup and water in a pan and bring to the boil. Reduce the heat and simmer for 10 minutes or until the apricots are soft. Allow to cool, transfer to a food processor or blender, and whizz until smooth.

2  In a bowl, toss together the melon, kiwi, grapes and stem ginger.

3  To serve, ladle some apricot smoothie on to the base of each plate or bowl and top with the gingery fruits. Serve at once.

# SPEEDY LIQUORICE SAUCE

*A quick version of liquorice custard using Pontefract cakes, which are easily available from supermarkets or confectioners.*

serves 4–6

> 425ml (15 fl oz) milk
> 115g (4 oz) liquorice Pontefract cakes, chopped into small pieces
> 150ml (5 fl oz) double cream

1 Place the milk and liquorice in a medium pan and gently heat until the liquorice has almost melted, stirring continuously.

2 Pour in the double cream and briefly stir to get a marbled effect. Serve at once.

# LEMONGRASS RICE PUDDING

*A simple baked rice pudding, infused with the subtle, zesty flavour of lemongrass.*

serves 4

> 65g (2½ oz) pudding rice
> 425ml (15 fl oz) milk
> 150ml (5 fl oz) double cream
> 25g (1 oz) caster sugar
> 1 large stick of lemongrass, cut in half lengthwise and bruised

1 Preheat the oven to 150°C/300°F/Gas Mark 2.

2 Lightly grease a shallow ovenproof dish.

3 In a bowl stir together the rice, milk, cream, sugar and lemongrass. Transfer to the prepared dish and cover with foil.

4 Bake in the preheated oven for 1¾ –2 hours until the rice is cooked.

# LIQUORICE CUSTARD/ICE-CREAM

*This liquorice custard can be served hot or cold, or chilled as an ice-cream, with fruit pies or crumbles or steamed puddings.*

serves 4

> 300ml (10 fl oz) milk
> 1 × 5cm (2 inch) piece of liquorice extract stick
> 300ml (10 fl oz) double cream
> 4 egg yolks
> 55g (2 oz) caster sugar

1 Heat the milk with the liquorice stick, very gently, until the stick has melted. Add the cream and very gently bring to the boil.

2 In a bowl, beat the egg yolks and sugar together. Remove the liquorice cream from the heat and gradually pour on to the yolks and sugar, stirring continuously. Strain the mixture back into a clean pan.

3 Return the pan to a very low heat and stir continuously until the mixture thickens enough to coat the back of a spoon, *but do not allow to boil.*

4 Serve warm or cold with your chosen dessert, or chill well and transfer to an ice-cream-maker or freezer until frozen.

# CANTALOUPE AND GINGER SAUCE

*Buy fresh, ready-made custard to whizz up this fab melon and ginger sauce. Especially good with* Rhubarb and Cardamom Pud *(see page 144).*

serves 4

> 400ml (14 fl oz) ready-made fresh custard
> 1 medium cantaloupe melon, peeled, de-seeded
>   and roughly chopped
> 3 pieces of stem ginger, roughly chopped

1 Simply place the ingredients in a blender or food processor and whizz until smooth.

# CASSIS AND CINNAMON BERRY SOUP

*This beautiful dessert soup can be made with any of the summer berries – strawberries, raspberries, blueberries, redcurrants...*

serves 4

450g (1 lb) mixed summer berries
200ml (7 fl oz) double cream, lightly whipped
4 good-quality shortbread biscuits

FOR THE SYRUP:
285g (10 oz) granulated sugar
600ml (1 pint) water
1 cinnamon stick
Cassis liqueur to taste

1 Place the sugar, water and cinnamon stick in a pan and gently heat until the sugar has dissolved. Bring to the boil and simmer for about 10 minutes until the liquid has become slightly syrupy. Remove from the heat and chill.

2 When cold, add the Cassis to the chilled syrup to taste.

3 To serve, arrange the berries on four serving plates or bowls. Spoon over the Cassis syrup and serve at once with double cream and shortbread biscuits.

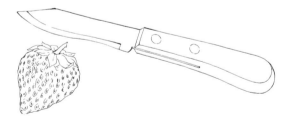

# HOT STRAWBERRY AND VANILLA DOMINOES

*Warm strawberries baked with vanilla sugar on a pastry base won't last long enough to play a game of dominoes!*

**makes 6**

55g (2 oz) caster sugar
1 vanilla pod, roughly chopped
350g (12 oz) ready-rolled puff pastry
approx. 30 medium-sized strawberries

1   Preheat the oven to 220°C/425°F/Gas Mark 7.

2   In a grinder or small food processor, place the sugar and vanilla pod, and whizz together well. Sieve into a bowl and set to one side.

3   Trim the pastry to form a rectangle 35 × 19cm (14 × 7½ inches). Cut the pastry into six strips measuring 6 × 19cm (2½ × 7½ inches) and place on a non-stick baking tray.

4   Prick the pastry bases well and sprinkle with half the vanilla sugar. Lay a single line of strawberries down the centre of each base and scatter over the remaining vanilla sugar.

5   Bake in the oven for 15 minutes until the pastry is risen and golden, and serve at once with cream or vanilla ice-cream.

# CLOVEY BREAD PUDDING

*A cross between a cake and traditional bread pudding. Cut into wedges and serve warm with vanilla ice-cream or custard, or cold as a spicy cake.*

serves 6–8

175g (6 oz) fresh white crusty bread, torn into small pieces

150 ml (5 fl oz) milk

85g (3 oz) dried ready-to-eat apricots, roughly chopped

85g (3 oz) dried ready-to-eat figs, roughly chopped

85g (3 oz) soft brown sugar

1 teaspoon cloves, dry-roasted and ground

2 tablespoons clear honey

grated rind of 1 orange

25g (1 oz) butter, melted

1 egg, beaten

1   Preheat the oven to 190°C/375°F/Gas Mark 5, and grease a 20cm (8 inch) shallow round cake tin.

2   Place the bread in a large bowl and pour over the milk. Leave to stand for 10 minutes.

3   Add the fruits, sugar, cloves, honey, grated orange rind, melted butter and egg. Squeeze and mix all the ingredients together and transfer to the prepared cake tin.

4   Bake in the oven for 45–50 minutes until firm and golden. Leave to stand in the tin for 10 minutes before turning out.

# index

ale, hot gingered 138
artichokes, with green beans and
    almonds 31
asparagus, saffron mayonnaise with 103
aubergines
    Aubergine and chickpea curry 126
    Aubergine, ginger and sesame
        tongues 46
    Cumin and aubergine mezze plate 77
    Skillet vegetables 106
avocado
    Avocado relish 137
    Black and red stew with 18
    Ginger sushi salad with avocado and
        sesame 40–1
    Pine Caesar salad 73

beans (pulses)
    Baked sweet potatoes with chilli sin
        carne 19
    Black and red stew with avocado and
        soured cream 18
    Fennel and fennel minestrone 62
    Juniper cassoulet 98
    Mustard and maple baked beans 72
    Mexican bean cakes 25
    Sichuan-dressed borlotti beans 96
beetroot
    Beetroot and dill pâté with tangy
        cucumber 70
    Horseradish latkes with 50
Black pepper pineapple 91
bread and rolls
    Brown mustard seed naan bread 141
    Cheshire caraway rustic rolls 65
    Chillied feta and ratatouille rolls 29
    Cornbread salad with fresh tomato
        sauce 16–17
    Cracked black pepper and figgy bread
        92
    Instant pittas 140
    Nutmeg and white cheese bread 113
    Spiced apple bread with honey butter
        107
    Tomato and fennel stew with garlic
        bread 61
bread pudding 157
breadsticks, mozzarella 96
broccoli
    Pappardelle pasta with lemongrass
        cream and 44–5
    Stir-fry, with mustard and orange
        pepper dressing 76
Brown mustard seed naan bread 141
butternut squash, cardamom-spiced 85
Butternut squash, potato, tamarind and
    coconut curry 88

butters, flavoured 107, 133

Cabbage with star anise and pear 89
Cantaloupe and ginger sauce 153
caraway rustic rolls, Cheshire 65
cardamom pods 8
    Cardamom and olive baked rice 81
    Cardamom and tomato spaghetti en
        papillote 82–3
    Cardamom-spiced butternut squash
        85
    Chilled cardamom mango 80
    Lettuce and pea soup with cardamom
        84
    Rhubarb and cardamom pud 144–5
    Sweet cardamom coffee and cream
        138
carrot cakes, savoury cumin 71
Cassis and cinnamon berry soup 154–5
cauliflower, curried, with paneer 118
Cayenne crisp tempura 32
Celeriac, carrot and horseradish
    remoulade 47
cheese
    Cheese and mace soufflés 114
    Chillied feta and ratatouille rolls 29
    Chillied thyme cheese 20–1
    Clove-grilled mandarins with Stilton
        108–9
    Cracked cumin tabbouleh pie 74–5
    Dolcelatte salad with ginger and
        apple dressing 43
    Garlic and chive pâté 21
    Garlic mushrooms with cheese and
        chive polenta 58
    Mozzarella breadsticks 96
    Nutmeg and white cheese bread 113
    Pink and green peppered halloumi 93
    Roasted Parmesan vegetables 28
    Savoury cumin carrot cakes with
        peppered cream cheese 71
    Skillet vegetables with a cheese sauce
        106
    Smoky paprika red risotto 34–5
    Spicy fruit chutney with cumin goat's
        cheese 119
    Tamarind, pear and date chutney on
        cheese on toast 86–7
chickpeas
    Aubergine and chickpea curry 126
    Indian pasties 63
    Lemon and paprika houmous with
        baked pimentos 36
Chillies 8–9, 15–36
    Chilli butter 133
    Chilli, coconut and lime Thai
        seasoning 135
    Chilli sin carne, baked sweet potatoes
        with 19
    Chilli sorbet with tequila 17
    Chillied eggs on crispy rocket salad
        26–7
    Chillied feta and ratatouille rolls 29
    Chillied thyme cheese 20–1
Chocolate and vanilla prune baked tart
    143

cinnamon 9
    Cassis and cinnamon berry soup
        154–5
    Cinnamon and honey vegetables 110
    Orange and cinnamon cookies 145
    Plum galette 148–9
    Spiced apple bread with honey butter
        107
    Skillet vegetables with cinnamon
        sauce 106
Citrus fruit soup 149
Clove-grilled mandarins with stilton
    108–9
Clovey bread pudding 157
coconut
    Butternut squash, potato, tamarind
        and coconut curry 88
    Chilli, coconut and lime Thai
        seasoning 135
    Coconut gravy 133
    Iced allspice and coconut creams
        144–5
    Risotto with coconut milk and saffron
        spinach 101
coffee, sweet cardamom 138
coriander 9
    Garlic, chilli, cashew and coriander
        seasoning 136
    Mushroom fidget pies with soured
        cream and coriander 68
    Sweet potato and coriander soup
        66–7
    Warm coriander seed tattie salad
        69
Cornbread salad with fresh tomato sauce
    16–17
courgettes
    Roasted courgette and lemongrass
        soup 54
    Saffron pasta paella 112
    Skillet vegetables 106
    Turmeric scramble with 39
    Warm galangal-dressed noodles 49
couscous, dressings for 134, 135, 136
cucumber
    Beetroot and dill pâté with tangy
        cucumber 70
    Tikka cucumber 127
cumin 9
    Cracked cumin tabbouleh pie 74–5
    Cumin and aubergine mezze plate 77
    Cumin, orange and garlic dressing
        134
    Indian pasties 63
    Savoury cumin carrot cakes 71
    Spicy fruit chutney with cumin goat's
        cheese 119
    Stuffed fiery beef tomatoes 117
curries
    Aubergine and chickpea 126
    Butternut squash, potato, tamarind
        and coconut 88
    Curried cauliflower and paneer 118
    Madras egg rösti 123
custards
    Cantaloupe and ginger sauce 153

Ginger and lime baked custards with passionfruit 150
Liquorice 152, 153

desserts 17, 20–1, 80, 91, 142–58
dill 9
Beetroot and dill pâté with tangy cucumber 70
Warm juniper and celeriac potatoes 97
Dolcelatte salad with ginger and apple dressing 43
dressings
ginger and apple 43
instant spicy 134–6
mustard and orange pepper 76
passionfruit vinaigrette 20
saffron mayonnaise 103
drinks 138–9

eggs
Cheese and mace soufflés 114
Chillied eggs on crispy rocket salad 26–7
Madras egg rösti 123
Spiced root vegetables with eggs and mango jam 128–9
Thai shiitake and ginger omelette 38
Turmeric scramble with courgettes 39

fennel 9
Fennel and fennel minestrone 62
Roasted parmesan vegetables 28
Tomato and fennel stew with garlic bread 61
fresh fruits, ginger, with apricot smoothie 151

Galangal-dressed noodles 49
garlic 10
Baked garlic onions with red wine gravy 52–3
Cumin, orange and garlic dressing 134
Garlic and chive pâté 21
Garlic bread, with tomato and fennel stew 61
Garlic, chilli, cashew and coriander seasoning 136
Garlic mushrooms with cheese and chive polenta 58
Garlic, pepper and tomato-dressed pasta 56
Garlic tzatziki 131
Lemon, parsley and garlic gremolata dressing 134
Roasted garlic sauce 57
Roasted red onion and garlic dressing 136
Spaghettini with chilli, garlic and basil 30
Vegetable stew with cashew and garlic picada 55
ginger 10
Aubergine, ginger and sesame tongues 46
Cantaloupe and ginger sauce 153

Dolcelatte salad with ginger and apple dressing 43
Ginger and lime baked custards with passionfruit 150
Ginger fresh fruits with apricot smoothie 151
Ginger sushi salad with avocado and sesame 40–1
Gingered nuts with black beans and rice 42
Gingered soba noodles with mushrooms 59
Hot gingered ale 138
Thai shiitake and ginger omelette 38
Gnocchi alla Milanese 104–5
Green beans, artichokes and salted cayenne almonds 31

Halloumi, pink and green peppered 93
horseradish 10
Celeriac, carrot and horseradish remoulade 47
Horseradish latkes with beetroot 50
Horseradish mash 132

Indian pasties 63

Jerk split peas with buttered black rice 122
juniper 10
Juniper and barley risi 99
Juniper cassoulet 98
Warm juniper and celeriac potatoes 97

Lemon and paprika houmous with baked pimentos 36
Lemon, parsley and garlic gremolata dressing 134
lemongrass 11
Lemongrass rice pudding 152
Pappardelle pasta with lemongrass cream 44–5
Roasted courgette with lemongrass soup 54
Lettuce and pea soup with cardamom 84
Liquorice custard/ice-cream 153
liquorice sauce, speedy 152

Madras egg rösti 123
mango
Chilled cardamom mango 80
Fresh mango jam 128–9
melon
Cantaloupe and ginger sauce 153
Ginger fresh fruits with apricot smoothie 151
Melon with peppered Parmesan 91
Mexican bean cakes 25
mixed spices, recipes with 116–29
Mozzarella breadsticks with Sichuan-dressed borlotti beans 96
mushrooms
Garlic, with cheese and chive polenta 58
Gingered soba noodles with 59

Mushroom fidget pies 68
Thai shiitake and ginger omelette 38
mustard 11
Brown mustard seed naan bread 141
Mustard and maple baked beans 72
Mustard, honey and butter mash 132
Pine Caesar salad 73
Stir-fry broccoli with mustard dressing 76
Stock check pie 78

noodles
Gingered soba, with mushrooms 59
Nutty, with wilted greens 124–5
Pad Thai 24
Warm galangal-dressed 49
Wasabi 48
nutmeg and mace 11
Cheese and mace soufflés 114
Nutmeg and banana toffee tart 146–7
Nutmeg and cream cheese mash 132
Nutmeg and onion batter pudding 111
Nutmeg and white cheese bread 113
Roasted pumpkin pasta with nutmeg 115
nuts
Garlic, chilli, cashew and coriander seasoning 136
Gingered, with black beans and rice 42
Nutty noodles with wilted greens 124–5
Vegetable stew with cashew and garlic picada 55

onions
Baked garlic onions with red wine gravy 52–3
Nutmeg and onion batter pudding 111
Roasted red onion and garlic dressing 136
oranges
Citrus fruit soup 149
Clove-grilled mandarin oranges with Stilton 108–9
Cumin, orange and garlic dressing 134
Orange and cinnamon cookies 145

Pad Thai noodles 24
Pappardelle pasta with lemongrass cream and broccoli 44–5
passionfruit
Ginger and lime baked custards with 150
Pawpaw and passionfruit vinaigrette 20
pasta
Cardamom and tomato spaghetti en papillote 82–3
dressings for 134, 136
Garlic, pepper and tomato-dressed 56
Pappardelle, with lemongrass cream and broccoli 44–5
Roasted pumpkin pasta with nutmeg 115
Saffron pasta paella 112

Spaghettini with chilli, garlic and basil 30

pâté, beetroot and dill, with tangy cucumber 70

pâté, garlic and chive 21

Pawpaw and passionfruit vinaigrette 20

pears
Cabbage with star anise and 89
Pine Caesar salad 73
Tamarind, pear and date chutney 86–7

pepper and peppercorns, recipes with 90–6

pies
Cracked cumin tabbouleh pie 74–5
Mushroom fidget pies 68
Stock check pie 78

Pine Caesar salad 73

pineapple, black pepper 91

pittas, instant, 140

pizza, open-roasted vegetable 22–3

Plum galette 148–9

polenta, cheese and chive, with garlic mushrooms 58

potatoes
Butternut squash, potato, tamarind and coconut curry 88
Crushed new potatoes with turmeric cream 51
Horseradish latkes with beetroot 50
Madras egg rösti 123
Real spiced chips 33
Saffron potato tortilla 102
Skillet vegetables 106
Slashed jerk potatoes 120–1
Spiced mash 132
Warm coriander seed tattie salad 69
Warm juniper and celeriac potatoes 97

pumpkin, roasted, with pasta and nutmeg 115

relishes and chutneys
Avocado relish 137
Chilli jam 28
Fresh mango jam 128–9
Nectarine and olive relish 21
Spicy fruit chutney with cumin goat's cheese 119
Tamarind, pear and date chutney 86–7
Tikka cucumber 127

Rhubarb and cardamom pud 144–5

rice
Cardamom and olive baked rice 81
dressings for 134, 135, 136
Ginger sushi salad with avocado and sesame 40–1
Gingered nuts with black beans and rice 42
Jerk split peas with buttered black rice 122
Risotto with coconut milk and saffron spinach 101
Smoky paprika red risotto 34–5
Spiced root vegetables 128–9
Thai shiitake and ginger omelette 38

rice pudding, lemongrass 152

saffron 12
Gnocchi alla Milanese 104–5
Risotto with coconut milk and saffron spinach 101
Saffron mayonnaise with asparagus 103
Saffron pasta paella 112
Saffron potato tortilla 102

salads
Chunky fruit and nut salad 114
Clove-grilled mandarins with stilton 108–9
Dolcelatte salad with ginger and apple dressing 43
Ginger sushi salad with avocado and sesame 40–1
Green beans, artichokes and almonds 31
Pine Caesar salad 73
Spinach and radicchio salad 113
Warm coriander seed tattie salad 69

sauces 16–17, 57, 106, 125

sesame seeds 12
Aubergine, ginger and sesame tongues 46
Ginger sushi salad with avocado and sesame 40–1
Seedy seasoning 135
Wasabi noodles 48

Sichuan-dressed borlotti beans 96

Sichuan ramiro peppers 94–5

soup
Cassis and cinnamon berry 154–5
Citrus fruit 149
Fennel and fennel minestrone 62
Lettuce and pea, with cardamom 84
Roasted courgette and lemongrass 54
Sweet potato and coriander, with Thai rouille 66–7

Spaghettini with chilli, garlic and basil 30

Spiced apple bread with honey butter 107

Spiced root vegetables with eggs and fresh mango jam 128–9

spices 8–13
storage and preparation 13–14

Spicy fruit chutney with cumin goat's cheese 119

spinach
Indian pasties 63
Risotto with coconut milk and saffron spinach 101
Spinach and radicchio salad 113

star anise, cabbage and pear with 89

starters
Aubergine, ginger and sesame tongues 46
Beetroot and dill pâté with tangy cucumber 70
Cardamom spiced butternut squash 85
Celeriac, carrot and horseradish remoulade 47
Chilled cardamom mango 80
Chilli sorbet with tequila 17

Chillied thyme cheese 20–1

Cumin and aubergine mezze plate 77

Dolcelatte salad with ginger and apple dressing 43

Garlic and chive pâté 21

Ginger sushi salad with avocado and sesame 40–1

Lemon and paprika houmous with baked pimentos 36

Melon with peppered Parmesan and rocket 91

Pawpaw and passionfruit vinaigrette 20

Pink and green peppered halloumi 93

Roasted parmesan vegetables 28

Stir-fry broccoli with mustard and orange pepper dressing 76

Stock check pie 78

Strawberry and vanilla dominoes 156

Sweet potato and coriander soup with Thai rouille 66–7

sweet potatoes, baked, with Chilli sin carne 19

tamarind 13
Butternut squash, potato, tamarind and coconut curry 88
Tamarind, pear and date chutney on cheese on toast 86–7

Thai chilli paste 131

Thai shiitake and ginger omelette 38

Tikka cucumber 127

tomatoes
Cardamom and tomato spaghetti en papillote 82–3
Cornbread salad with fresh tomato sauce 16–17
Garlic, pepper and tomato-dressed pasta 56
Stuffed fiery beef tomatoes 117
Tomato and fennel stew with garlic bread 61
Tomato salad 104

turmeric 13
Crushed new potatoes with turmeric cream 51
Turmeric mash 132
Turmeric scramble with courgettes 39

vanilla 13
Chocolate and vanilla prune baked tart 143
Hot strawberry and vanilla dominoes 156

vegetable pizza, open roasted 22–3

Vegetable stew with cashew and garlic picada 55

vegetables, roasted Parmesan, with easy-peasy chilli jam 28

vegetables, skillet, with a cheese and cinnamon sauce 106

Vegetarian sausages 64

Wasabi noodles 48